# It's All Sorted

**A Business Owner's 9-Step Guide to Master Your Tax & Achieve Peace of Mind**

## Ben Walker

# Client Endorsements

*"Ben has been our accountant and a trusted business adviser for my group of companies for around 9 years. His unwavering commitment, together with his amazing Inspire team, have assisted our business in a broad range of areas, including cash flow, tax, structures, and some international tax matters. What makes Ben unique and awesome is his genuine passion for my business success and his ability to advise on generating family wealth. I am excited for the results that readers of It's All Sorted will have. It will give you the potential to achieve more, simply by investing the time to read, absorb and implement the principles Ben shares."*

Steve C

*"I have been an Inspire client for over 7 years. It has been a great comfort to know that I have had Ben and his team in my corner. I love that Inspire are not solely interested in the financial health of my business, but that it is ingrained in their DNA to take a wholistic and proactive view of business as being a vehicle to support the wellbeing and flourishing of my whole family. Ben and his team are knowledgeable, approachable, efficient, and dare I say, fun."*

Nathan D

*"I met Ben just after he started his business, which was fortuitous timing for me. I was really dissatisfied with the traditional accounting model I'd experienced at both small and big firms. Me always chasing them for assistance and them charging me by the minute.*

*Ben opened my eyes up to how accountants should operate. The Inspire team is transparent, responsive, and extremely proactive. They are always prodding me to look ahead and take action months in advance of tax and business deadlines, and they are happy to discuss all kinds of business and investment strategies to help guide decision making.*

*But Ben and his team's real superpower is their ability to empower clients to understand their numbers and take financial responsibility for themselves. This has been life changing for me and my family, and we are incredibly grateful for all of their assistance and support."*

**Bob N**

*"Embarking on our journey in our construction business, securing land, and building our family home seemed like an overwhelming challenge. However, Ben and the Inspire team in its infancy brought a genuine sense of care, thoughtfulness, gratitude, and guidance to the table. Previously, we had dealt with large accounting firms that made promises but required significant assistance from us, turning what we now recognize as simple tasks into complex endeavours.*

*Over the course of our 10-year business journey, filled with both triumphs and challenges, the unwavering constant has been the Inspire team. They transformed our approach to accounting, making it a self-sufficient service with occasional prompts for action and encouragement. Without delving into the intricate details, I can attest that having them by our side allows us to focus on building our future seamlessly. Expanding our investment portfolio, acquiring our warehouse, purchasing vehicles, navigating various business structures (some we weren't even aware we needed), and rebranding have become remarkably easy and stress-free.*

*The impact of Ben and his team, who embody softness, caring, and family values in everything they do, has been profound. Their influence has shaped our path in unimaginable ways. I wouldn't alter a thing in the next 10 years unless Ben suggests it—such is the trust we have in his expertise.*

*I wholeheartedly recommend this book to anyone aspiring to start a business, build a team, or simply strive for positive change. The strategies outlined are straightforward yet incredibly effective, allowing you to rest assured that everything is well taken care of.*

*Ben truly has it "All sorted" for us. His approach is a game-changer."*

**Kenny M**

Dedicated to my beautiful family – Stevie, Rose, Ezra & Poppy.

Always remember: we all have the power to create a life (and business) that gives us the ability to put our family first.

# Table of Contents

# Table of Contents

# Table of Contents

# Introduction:
## Not All Accountants Are Created Equal

In the lead up to starting Inspire, it was my vision to build an accounting firm that was built from the clients' perspective. What did this look like? It meant an accounting firm that billed fairly, delivered immense value, and was friendly to interact with. On the point of our company's value, it took us a couple of years to work out, but we started to measure the impact that we had on our clients' lives.

Being accountants, one of the things we were measuring was the dollars of tax savings that we saved. In the 2016 financial year, we launched our first "Save $500,000 Tax" campaign. In the lead up to 30 June 2016, we went about our ordinary tax planning service for our clients, but we added one thing: we tracked the amount of estimated tax they would have paid had they not used our tax planning service, and then we compared this to their estimated tax after they used our tax planning. This difference or 'tax saving' we shared with each client and added it to our tax saving tally.

We also tracked tax savings for potential clients where we reviewed their previous financial year's completed tax returns to check if their accountant had incorporated every legal tax strategy available to them. If there were strategies that the accountant missed, we calculated the difference in overpaid tax and discussed this with the potential client.

We had done tax planning and the tax review service for the 3 financial years prior to this, and I had done this service at the firm I had previously worked with. However, I had never properly tracked the number of tax savings per client or calculated it to a firm level. The goal of the "Save $500,000 Tax" campaign was to tally up our tax savings across the whole client base during our tax planning season. The season ran from early April to the 30th of June. The results were astounding.

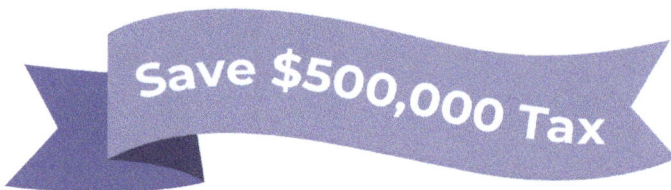

**Save $500,000 Tax**

The $500,000 goal we had set was massive, in my opinion, and it was a number that I thought would be extremely hard to hit. However, the number that we did hit (and after we had completed all our clients tax planning as well as onboarded some new clients throughout that process) was a grand total of $1.26 million.

At the time, this was an average of $18,000 in tax savings per client. Our average client paid us around

$6,000 in accounting fees per year, which meant that clients received approximately three times ROI on our accounting fees for the year. From that point onwards, we became known as a firm with the ability to make a measurable impact on our clients' lives, saving them an obscene amount of money.

Fast forward to 2023, and this year we hit a running total of $25 million of tax savings across our client base since we started tracking in 2016. It's hard to comprehend the volume of this impact, and it seems surreal thinking back to when I started Inspire with the original vision of making tangible improvements to my clients' lives.

This is because I started Inspire on my own with only a handful of clients in a 9-square-metre office with a rented printer and a MacBook Pro. Now, we are a team of over 20 in our Brisbane office, working with over 300 family business owners, and saving our new and existing clients millions of dollars of tax every financial year.

The purpose of this book is to share several of the strategies that have allowed us to save our clients this amount of money in tax. You'll also get some answers to our clients' most commonly asked questions when it comes to the basics around tax, dealing with the ATO, business structuring, and asset protection.

## What most accountants get wrong (learnings from saving $25M in tax+)

One question you might be asking yourself right now is, "How could you really save that much tax?" At Inspire, we offer prospective clients a "Look Under the Hood" process, which is a second opinion on their tax. One of the things we look for is if there are any tax saving opportunities that have been missed.

When it's boiled down, there are a handful of commonly missed tax saving strategies that cost business owners thousands or tens of thousands of dollars a year.

Those strategies that are commonly missed or not applied correctly are:

- Paying tax on money you haven't received yet
- Claiming depreciation correctly
- Using a trust (properly)
- Ensuring family members are in the same tax bracket
- Distributing to a bucket company
- Salaries paid to business owners
- Prepayments prior to 30 June
- Contributions to superannuation

There are more than the strategies in this above that have contributed to our tax savings tally, but by far these are the ones that are most commonly messed up when we are reviewing other accountants' work.

Plus there are other ways to save clients mega dollars, through restructuring their business or carefully applying small business capital gains tax concessions when they are selling a business.

My point here is that you must as a business owner be using an accountant with an awareness and a knack for saving you heaps of tax. Otherwise, there is a fairly high chance you'll be tipping the government tax you otherwise would not have had to pay.

## 10 reasons your accountant is a dinosaur

Here is a handful of reasons why I feel that most accountants are still stuck in the old way of accounting, or what we call a "dinosaur accountant".

## 1. They charge by the hour

I feel in most situations charging by the hour hurts the customer more than it helps. It also encourages the accountant to spend more time doing the work and being slow, instead of getting a great outcome for a client and delivering the work quickly and efficiently. I recommend looking for an accountant with fixed, clear, and transparent pricing that you agree with up front before the service starts.

## 2. They are not proactive

We hear the word "proactive" a lot when it comes to what prospective clients are looking for in an accountant. I often see a lack of proactivity, with clients often asking the accountant what to do and constantly following up. They're often looking in the rear-view mirror along with the accountant rather than looking forward with advisory or tax planning.

This does not mean that accountants should be mind readers, but rather they should have systems in place to have discussions about, for example, tax planning in the quarter before 30 June so that any advice could be implemented before the financial year finishes.

Proactivity is also reaching out to the client when they need to start the ball rolling on their tax, their BAS, bookkeeping, or other lodgements that are needed. And if the accountant notices any changes to the business that require a different direction in strategy, they should flag that with the client.

## 3. They send you surprise bills

Surprise bills suck. I had a client called Bob who came onboard in the early days of Inspire. He called me after I'd met him at an event I hosted, and he let me know that his accountant had taken him out for a lunch. They had caught up like mates, he had asked him how life is, how the family are going, and so on. He then asked a few questions about how Bob was doing with his business. He then went back to the office and promptly sent Bob a bill.

That's a pretty extreme example of a surprise bill. Bob didn't expect this at all, given that he thought he was just having a catch-up over lunch, but there are plenty of other examples I've heard of accountants sending surprise bills. This is usually when the accountant hasn't been clear that something they are going to do is going to cost the client money.

The surprise could even be in the amount of the bill, where they have quoted $3000 to do the work, and then it's turned out to be $7000, based on "additional time spent". The outcome would be slightly more palatable if the accountant had reached out when the time spent was at $3000, then giving the client an updated estimate of what the final price is likely to be.

## 4. They are slow to respond

This is one of the main reasons why people leave accountants. I struggled to get a response within days, weeks, or even months. One of our key performance indicators from very early in inspire was a 24-hour turnaround time responding to emails or phone calls from our clients.

We're definitely not perfect at this, but we realise that this communication is important to keeping our clients happy and relaxed. The other expectation to set is not every question can be answered quickly. If this is the case, a simple response saying something like, "I'll need to get back to you tomorrow or the next day on this question," is much better than just leaving a question unanswered for two or three days.

## 5. They just do the tax

If your accountant just does the tax returns, they are limited in their scope in providing value to the business and the family group doing more than just meeting lodgement deadlines. (By "family group" I mean all the individuals, companies and trusts that are owned or controlled by that family.)

I believe an accountant who works with business owners needs to do additional advisory work around tax planning, identify other financial services that the client needs (such as bookkeeping or mortgage broking) and would know who to refer to if the client has more advanced requirements, such as mergers and acquisitions, as an example.

## 6. They are not tech savvy

This point has fewer excuses, especially in more recent times. When I started in accounting, we used in-house servers that hosted extremely large software programmes that took a long time to run and were very slow when you were using them. What is awful for the client (especially when their accountant charges by the hour) is that you're paying an hourly rate for someone's expertise, and they're getting slowed down by software. We now have access to well-built, cloud-based software that helps us do what we need with our clients: there's no excuse for having old-school crappy software or using slow servers.

## 7. You have to push them to get things done

A sign that your accountant is struggling is when you are constantly following them up for work they should be delivering, you're the one suggesting ways to save tax or how things should be structured, or the questions that you've asked go unanswered. They may be overwhelmed, but if it's up to you to push the accountant for an answer, this can cost you money if you're not exactly sure what to do and when.

## 8. They're not entrepreneurial

Again, this one is relevant for business owners as clients — you can have a great accountant technically, but they may not be great at running a business. If that is the case, your technical questions and advice you receive from your accountant may be superb, but your client experience and interactions with the accounting firm may be quite poor, leading to frustrating relationships. The other outcome of not having an entrepreneurial accountant is that there is limited inspiration that you can take from them. Their mindset also might not match yours, potentially leading to advice that doesn't necessarily match your values.

## 9. They charge when you ask questions

If there's one way to kill a relationship, it's to charge money for every single email, phone call, and interaction that an accountant has with the client. That discourages you, as the client, from reaching out to your accountant to ask a question, with the fear that you may get another bill as a result. This means you could end up guessing what the answer to the question is and winging it, all because you'd prefer to not get the bill. Keep in mind, though this may cost you more money in the long run if your own research did not achieve the best outcome.

## 10. They don't give you proactive tax savings

One of the things I'm passionate about (because accountants often mess this up) is making sure the business owner pays the right amount of tax, and not a cent more. If you have an accountant that does not do tax planning before 30 June or does not have a focus on strategies you can use to reduce your tax, then I would be concerned that they are costing you not only their accounting fees but in missed tax savings as well. So how much should a good accountant charge?

"You pay peanuts, you get monkeys" is a saying my good friend and financial planner Nick Webb has said to me over the years. This is usually when we're surprised at how low some of the fees other professionals are charging (and often more shocked at the outcomes to the client as a result).

But I do truly believe, in life, you get what you pay for. The same applies for accountants. You shouldn't look for the cheapest – unless you want crap, reactive, and limited help. I also don't believe you should just go and find the most expensive either.

We work with small business owners, and my recommendation is that you need an adviser that works proactively throughout the financial year to help you get your tax sorted and regularly offers proactive advice. They should also be able to provide advice that is reactive to your requests throughout the year. This sort of adviser, at a bare minimum, should cost a few thousand dollars.

At Inspire, we have a package called "It's All Sorted" — a proactive tax and accounting subscription that aims to pay for itself with tax savings. We charge from around the $7,900+GST mark for a standard small business, which includes the personal tax returns of up to 2 individuals in the family group.

The price increases based on what we call the structures or entities in the family group (such as companies and trusts), but also the complexity of the industry, turnover, employees, and many other factors.

If you have an accountant who "just does the tax" – their starting price might be between $2,500 and $3,000 on the lower end. But this isn't comparing apples and apples: that sort of comparison between a "just the tax" accountant and our "It's All Sorted" is apples and oranges.

So, my recommendation is if you're a business owner whose business is growing, who appreciates good advice, who wants to make sure they pay the right amount of tax and not a cent more, you'll need to invest at least $5,000 (though likely more) to get the sort of advice that is right for you.

# PART 1:

# The Basics – Getting Organised (And Staying Out Of Jail!)

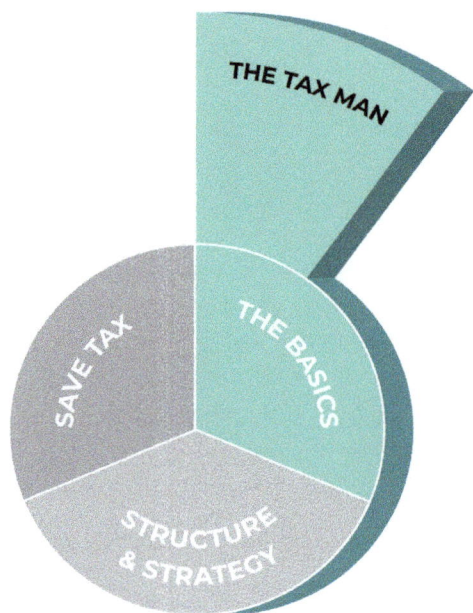

THE TAX MAN

THE BASICS

SAVE TAX

STRUCTURE & STRATEGY

# Chapter 1:
## The Tax Man (Everything you need to know with the ATO)

*"Death and taxes may be certain, but it's often said that the Tax Man is more punctual."*

**ANONYMOUS**

This chapter is all about the ATO: how to deal with them and what your obligations are to them. However, if you are a seasoned business owner and know your obligations for your family group backwards, I won't judge if you skim read or flick through these next few pages with the super basic stuff in it.

## Shift your relationship with tax

I want to share three ideas that may change your mindset or relationship with tax. I often speak to business owners, and they have a very negative view of tax. I don't love paying it either, but there are some positives to paying it. I also believe that if you have a positive relationship with paying taxes, it makes running and growing your business easier.

### I want you to pay $250,000 in tax each year

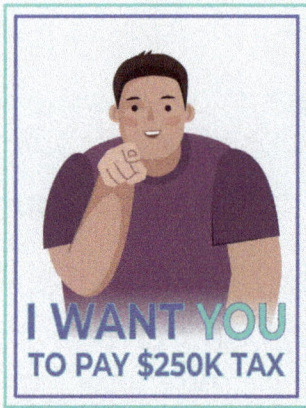
I WANT YOU
TO PAY $250K TAX

About a year into running Inspire, I met a coach who used to run an accounting firm. He told me that he used to tell his clients that he wanted them to pay a minimum of $250,000 in tax each year. When he mentioned this to me, I almost fell off my chair. I instantly thought, is this guy nuts?!

As we chatted, I worked out that this encouragement was not necessarily to pay tax for the sake of paying tax, but to be paying $250,000 worth of tax meant that the client is likely earning $1,000,000 or more.

That is something aspirational and paying that amount of taxes is part of earning $1,000,000. Therefore, I would love *all* of our clients to be paying $250,000 or more in tax, assuming that amount is the correct amount of tax for that client.

The other thing this point addresses is the reluctance of people to "make a profit" in business because they are worried about paying tax — that to me doesn't make logical sense. If the goal is to not make profit, then you actually have no, or minimal financial benefit from your business, and therefore the business likely has very limited value if you were to sell it.

So lean into making profit, and assuming your structure is right and you've got a good accountant who does tax planning, your business should provide a good income for your family and ideally be built so that it has value in the event of a sale.

## Where did the tax go?

The other thing to think about is where our tax ends up going. Years ago, on your notice of assessment (an ATO document issued after you lodge your personal tax return), they used to include a breakdown of where your taxes ended up. This was in a graph format, so if you paid $20,000 in tax for that year, it showed where your dollars actually ended up in the different public services that are provided in Australia, eg the allocation of money that went to healthcare, social security, defence, and so on.

Now, I don't necessarily agree with everything that the government does or spends "our" money on, but I do believe we have a relatively safe country with good health care available, a high standard of education, and other public services that serve the population. So it takes the edge off paying tax when I think that some of this money is going back into things I use or get benefits from.

## Getting paid in cash is not a tax saving strategy

I feel I've got to address this one pretty early on in the book. I'm not advocating for doing anything illegal to save tax and that includes taking cash payments in your business. From my perspective, doing this is shooting yourself in your foot for the following reasons:

1. Instead of paying income tax, you end up paying what I call "sleep at night tax" — where your brain resources are tied up in making sure you don't get caught taking cash or that you're ever get caught out in the future.

2. When business owners get loans from banks, the banks look at their financial statements and tax returns to see how much income is coming into the business. If you're taking cash, this income won't be looked at by the banks, and it will prevent you from getting the maximum loan you could with your total income had you declared it.

3. It also affects the value of your business. Buyers will review your financial statements, management reports, and tax returns through the due diligence process to make sure you are complying with your obligations and what your expected future earnings should be from your business. If you have cash payments that aren't showing in these, that will reduce the value of your business and potentially give red flags to a buyer.

## What do you need to lodge?

The first thing to consider is what you'll need to be lodging for your business and family group. In the ATO's eyes, every entity has its own lodgement requirements. This means that you'll have different lodgement requirements for:

- Individuals

- Companies

- Trusts

- Self-managed super funds

- Partnerships

- Any other variation of the entities listed above that you have a tax file number or Australian business number for

Most entities at minimum will need to lodge a tax return. Entities registered for GST will need to lodge a BAS either on a monthly, quarterly, or annual basis, depending on their registration. Generally, when we refer to annually, it is the financial year from 1 July to 30 June the following year.

Entities registered for fringe benefits tax also need to lodge a fringe benefits tax return ("FBT"), which is a different year compared to a financial year. The FBT year goes from 1 April through to 31 March the following year.

These lodgements have a due date requirement, and it also depends on who lodges the document, because if a tax agent lodges a tax return or a quarterly BAS, there are extensions available that are automatically applied because a tax agent lodged it.

Most business owners will need an annual set of tax returns for their whole group. If you're a small to medium business, your business will likely lodge a quarterly BAS and, potentially, a monthly instalment activity statement or IAS. All of these lodgements need appropriate records to be kept so that accountants and bookkeepers can prepare the relevant things that need to be lodged.

## Different lodgements you might need

Let's run through in a bit of detail the different types of documents you might need to prepare and lodge with the ATO.

### Annual Tax Returns & Financials

#### What is it?

Your annual tax return is used to tell the ATO how much taxable income you have earned in the financial year, as well as how much income tax will be due for that entity. Every entity that earns income, runs a business, or has investments needs to lodge a tax return. This includes you as individuals and any companies or trusts you have – even your Self Managed Super Fund ("SMSF").

The tax return includes more than just the taxable income; however, the remaining information is more disclosure information that the ATO uses to check the information you reported v industry benchmarks, how to categorise the size of your business (ie your revenue), and also other key disclosure items that are important for the ATO to see.

Financial statements are prepared based on your accounting information and are usually a requirement for having a trust or a company that runs a business or invests. For most small businesses, these statements aren't required to be lodged directly with the ATO or ASIC.

But they are used and required to fill out parts of the tax return, like the balance sheet and other disclosure items, like certain loans. The banks will also want to see financial statements for your entities if you go to acquire finance for your business or home lending.

## When is it due?

Your tax return due date depends on a few things:

- Whether you lodge your return or if a tax agent lodges it for you

- The entity type (individual, company, trust, SMSF)

- The taxpayer class (as determined by the ATO)

- If it was set up during the current financial year (ie a "new" entity) or it has previously lodged

- If the previous tax return was lodged late

As a general guide, most small business owners' group tax returns are due on the 15th of May – this is almost a full year after the financial year ends. Bigger groups or higher taxpayers may be due on 31st March.

If the entities were lodged late the prior year or have overdue returns, the tax returns are generally due by 31st October, leaving only 4 months to lodge after the year ends. To be sure, it is worth getting your accountant to confirm when each of your entities and personal tax returns are due so there are no surprises.

## What is the process?

I thought it would be good to share the process of what the accounting firm does to prepare your financial statements and tax returns. They are ordinarily all prepared at the same time as every entity and individuals in your family group. Here are the high-level steps to prepare it:

i. Your bookkeeping for the relevant periods needs to be finalised.

ii. The accountant prepares an initial query list.

iii. You send your initial documents in response.

iv. They process that first round and draft your financials and tax return, usually for your whole group.

v. Your accountant may send a further list of information for any remaining questions they have as they process your returns to draft stage.

vi. You answer any remaining questions.

vii. Your accountants finalise the returns.

viii. Ideally, you have a meeting with your accountant to discuss the returns and anything to keep in mind moving forward. At Inspire, we call this an annual 'AGM'.

## Quarterly / Monthly BAS

### What is it?

Your business activity statement or BAS is a statement that is prepared for businesses every quarter or month, depending on their registration cycle. It reports the high-level sales and expenses and the GST that is owed or refundable with the ATO. A business needs to pay any GST they have received from customers to the ATO, and they also can claim GST they paid to suppliers throughout the relevant BAS period.

The BAS can include other tax obligations on the same statement, such as PAYG Withholding from salaries, PAYG tax instalments and even other taxes depending on the business.

### When is it due?

If it is a quarterly BAS, the BAS is due the 28th of the month following the end of the quarter. So if it is the September quarter, it will ordinarily be due 28th October. If a tax agent lodges it, there is an additional 4 weeks the BAS has to be lodged.

If it is a monthly BAS, the BAS is due 21 days into the following month. So September monthly BAS would be due 21st October.

### What is the process?

- Your bookkeeping for the relevant period needs to be finalised.
- The BAS preparer (sometimes the business owner, which is not ideal, or a bookkeeper or an accounting

firm) runs the relevant BAS reports, checks over the reports for accuracy, then prepares a BAS.

- BAS is then sent for review and signing by the business owner.

- BAS is lodged with ATO and payment should be made by the due date.

## IAS

### What is it?

Your instalment activity statement or IAS is a statement that is prepared to be lodged with the ATO. It only reports Pay As You Go (PAYG) withholding from salaries paid to employees of the business, and it is often used if the BAS cycle is quarterly. But the business's PAYG withholding cycle is more frequent, such as monthly. No GST is reportable on an IAS, otherwise it would be called monthly BAS.

### When is it due?

Often, we see this as a monthly statement, and it is due 21 days into the month following the month in which the IAS relates to. So an August IAS would be ordinarily due 21st September.

### What is the process?

- Because an IAS only covers PAYG withholding, only the payroll needs to be finalised for the period in which the IAS relates to.

- Appropriate reports are run from the payroll software, then reviewed, and the IAS is filled out.

- IAS is lodged with the ATO and payment should be made by the due date.

## PAYG Instalments

### What is it?

Pay as you go instalments, or PAYG instalments, are different from PAYG withholding mentioned above. The difference is that PAYG instalments are quarterly pre-payments of estimated income tax for the entity that is issued with a PAYG instalment notice. PAYG withholding is the actual tax that is withheld from employees of an entity during the payroll process.

PAYG instalment notices are issued to entities that receive untaxed income, such as business income or investment income with no franked portions (franked being a portion of tax credits attached to investment income).

If the entity receiving the PAYG instalment believes that the amount of withholding is too much or too little, the entity may lodge a variation of PAYG instalment with the ATO. Paying more than the notice is acceptable. However, do bear in mind that if you pay less than the ATO estimated amount, there may be a tax bill at the end of the year as a result of the entity varying it lower, which can sometimes result in interest and penalties from the ATO. I have heard of this, but I have never witnessed it in my 17+ year career.

### When is it due?

The PAYG instalment notices are usually issued quarterly and due 28 days after the quarter finished. So a September quarter PAYG instalment notice is usually due 28th October.

## What is the process?

Unless the taxpayer wishes to vary the instalment amount, there is nothing to do apart from pay the PAYG notice amount by the due date.

If the entity wishes to vary the amount, it must fill out the form and lodge by the due date because variations received after the due date are declined.

## FBT Tax Return

## What is it?

A fringe benefits tax (FBT) return declares and remits fringe benefits that have been provided to employees of an entity throughout the FBT year.

The FBT year runs from 1st April to the following 31st March, so it is not the ordinary financial year.

Fringe benefits are benefits provided to employees, their families, or other associates, and can include things such as access to company vehicles, team entertainment, gifts, parties, holidays, providing access to paid parking near the office, and many others.

There are very detailed tax laws around what falls in and out of the requirement to be taxed on these benefits. For instance, a laptop provided for an employee that is used mainly for work purposes falls under an exemption of portable electronic devices. Whereas if you purchased a

TV for an employee's house, and there's zero or hardly any requirement from a work perspective to have that, it would be a taxable fringe benefit and tax would need to be paid.

The FBT tax return is where you declare all of these benefits and the associated fringe benefits tax that is payable on it.

### When is it due?

The fringe benefits tax return is due 21st May if the entity lodges it itself, or generally 25th of June if a tax agent lodges for the entity.

### What is the process?

- Your FBT requirements need to be discussed in detail (if you have any).

- Documentation around the benefits provided needs to be provided to the accountant preparing the return.

- The return is prepared and sent for signing by the business owner.

- The return is lodged with the ATO, and the payment should be made by the due date.

## STP Finalisation

### What is it?

An STP finalisation, or Single Touch Payroll finalisation, is when you submit your declaration for payroll records to the ATO for the financial year. If you report and finalise your employee's information through an STP, you do not need to provide them payment summaries or lodge a payment summary annual report. (These were the old things to do before STP was brought in.)

Once this information is lodged, your employees will be able to access their information required for their tax return directly from the ATO or via their myGov account.

### When is it due?

Your STP finalisation is due by 14th of July each year for information that relates to the prior financial year which ended 30th June, so you have 14 calendar days to get this lodged.

### What is the process?

Your payroll software, such as Xero, will make this process fairly easy.

You'll just follow the prompts to confirm information, run required reports to double check the information you're about to submit to the ATO, then use the software to submit the information.

## The Top 4 ATO correspondences you might receive .

There are many types of letters that the ATO can send out throughout a financial year. Keep in mind as a business owner, these could apply to your different entities. The ATO sees each individual, trust, company, super fund as a separate entity to deal with for tax purposes, so each one is treated as a separate relationship they need to manage. Their main communication is through letters

and notices sent either digitally to the tax agent or an individual's myGov account or to the mailing address that is listed for the entity with the ATO.

I'll run through the four main types of correspondence that you might see from the ATO. These things are not exhaustive but rather the most common. They are in addition to the number of forms or correspondence sent for the different types of obligations listed in the previous section on lodgements.

## Notice of Assessment

This notice (NOA) is issued once your tax return has been lodged, and then the ATO assesses your tax payable or refundable. Only individuals receive them, other entities do not. They will have a calculation of what your taxable income is and how your tax payable or refundable is calculated. If you have a refund, it should let you know how that refund is going to be paid to you. If you have a payable, it will have payment details along with a due date on the notice.

## Statement of Account

This is basically a bank statement equivalent that is sent showing the transactions on certain accounts that you or your entity has with the ATO. It will show the debits and credits (amount owing or receivable) of your or your entity's account with the ATO. If there is an amount owing, it should clearly show the amount payable and the due date — along with payment details for it.

If there are penalties and interest showing on your statement, you or your tax agent can apply to the ATO for these to be remitted in special circumstances. Apart from the time and energy for the remission application, there are no other downsides to applying for it — it's just up to the ATO whether they grant the remission or not.

## Division 293 Notice

A Division 293 is a notice for an extra tax that is payable on superannuation contributions if the individual has a Division 293 income of more than the current threshold of $250,000. The Division 293 income is a modified calculation, but it is based firstly on taxable income.

The extra Division 293 tax is charged at 15% of the excess over $250,000 of the Division 293 income and super contributions, or 15% on the concessional super contributions if your Division 293 income is already over $250,000. A simple way of looking at is as an additional 15% tax on your super contributions if you're earning over $250,000.

## Correspondence to do with debt

There are many different types of letters the ATO will send out when they are attempting to recover tax debt owed to them. I'll cover the process of this in a bit more detail in Chapter 3. For now, the goal is to not ignore these notices – they will ramp up in tone, and if no action is taken, this will result in more and more recovery action. The earlier you deal with something related to the ATO, the more reasonable they will be in trying to reach agreements that sort out debt repayments, such as a payment plan.

## ASIC Statements, records & register to keep up to date

In Australia, when you register a company, the company will need to interact with the Australian Securities and Investment Commission (ASIC). The ASIC looks after the registration, information, and regulation when it comes to companies. This even includes private companies that you as a small business owner trade out of, or even companies that only act as trustees of trusts or trustees of super funds.

Here's some things to keep in mind about the ASIC.

### Director's Identification Number

A Director's Identification Number or DIN is a unique identifier assigned to everyone who has verified their information with the Australian Business Registry Services. It was something brought in over the past few years to reduce the chance of fraud or illegal phoenixing that was happening. Illegal phoenixing is where an entity with usually high debts or liabilities sells its assets to another usually related entity at less than market value and liquidates the original entity.

To set up a company now, all directors must have a DIN ready and supplied to whomever is registering that company.

To apply for a DIN, you'll need to:

1. Set up a myGovID if you don't already have one (myGovID is different to myGov)

2. Gather required documents for ID verification

3. Complete your application

## Annual Company Statement

After registration, each year the ASIC will send you an invoice for the annual renewal of the company. They do this around 2 months before the registration date. The Annual Company Statement fee is currently $310 for a normal proprietary company, and it is currently $63 for a special purpose company (proprietary), such as the trustee of an SMSF.

If you fail to pay this on time, the current late fees are:

- Up to 1 month late $93

- More than 1 month late $387 (this is more than the fee in the first place!)

These fees are indexed each year.

Also, the ASIC are not reasonable like the ATO when it comes to remission of penalties and fines – I've never heard of these being remitted with the ASIC, even in cases where there is no way it was the fault of the company. So I recommend paying these when you receive the invoice or at least set up the payment, so it's automatic a few days before it is due.

## Business Names

Business name registrations have been coordinated with the ASIC for the past few years. Previously, it was a state-based system. The ASIC system is called ASIC Connect. A business name provides permission to 'trade as' a name that isn't the same as the legal entity.

For instance, if I ran Inspire Accountants as a sole trader (which I wouldn't for many reasons, but let's just imagine it for a sec), I would need a trading name registered to my personal name. So, legally, I would be Benjamin Walker, trading as Inspire Accountants. If I had Inspire Accountants Pty Ltd, I would not need a business name to trade with the name Inspire Accountants Pty Ltd, given it is the name of the company.

We recommend the business names are registered via the business owner's account with the ASIC. We liken it like a domain registration — preferably you're in control of that login. The other benefit is we do not need to charge a fee for the registration. You'll just need to make sure you register the business name to the correct entity.

## Forms to change company details

The final key interaction I feel worth noting that you'll have with the ASIC is forms relating to changes in your company.

This can include:

- Adding directors
- Removing directors
- Updating addresses (super common)
- Transferring shares
- Issuing shares
- Deregistering a company

Basically, there's heaps of changes you may need to make to a company at various stages of the company's life cycle. There are many types of forms for the ASIC, and they are numbered forms for reference to what they do.

Most (not all) of the changes to companies are actually dealt with using form 484. I've been doing these since the 2000s! Additionally, please note that late fees also apply to late lodgement of certain forms where there are requirements to notify the ASIC of the change to the company details within a certain timeframe from the change occuring.

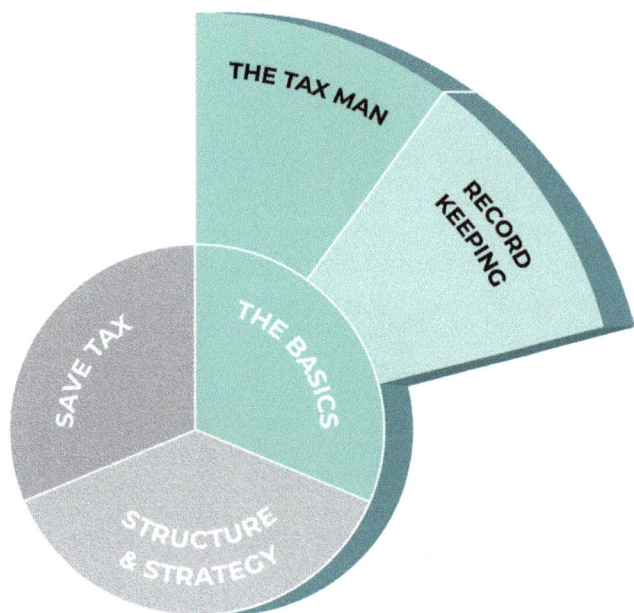

THE TAX MAN

RECORD KEEPING

THE BASICS

SAVE TAX

STRUCTURE & STRATEGY

# Chapter 2:
## Record Keeping

*"Bookkeeping may seem like a humble task, but in the world of taxes, it's the map that guides you through a labyrinth of deductions and compliance."*

**Sarah Reynolds**

Here I'm going to share the very basics of what is required as a business owner to lodge and pay. If you're a seasoned business owner, you may want to either skim read or skip this chapter as it may be very familiar with you already. But maybe you need to brush up on some of these points to make it run like clockwork. There may be a distinction that you do not know. You could even read it from a perspective of, how can I do it even better in this area?

## The Power of Xero

When I started in accounting, the market leading software provider was MYOB. I used my it at my first job at a Big Four accounting firm, and even in my second job in a

smaller suburban practice — MYOB had a massive hold on the Australian business market and also Australian accounting firms.

While Xero was started in 2006, I didn't hear about it until around 2011. The concept of a cloud accounting software was pretty foreign, let alone its ability to run accounting firm practices from the software as well. Since the early days, Xero has gotten better and better with their features, offering accountant-specific software to help with lodgements and dealing with the ATO.

Here's some points of why accountants in business owners love Xero:

### 1. Shared portal with your accountant

This first point was mind-blowing at the time — the concept of a shared portal or a shared ledger with the accountant and the client having simultaneous access.

Previously what used to happen is the accountant would look at the record-keeping of the client, typically in MYOB or QuickBooks, and then import this information into the accounting practice's software, usually manually, while charging hourly rates to do this.

For accounting firms who prepare their clients' documents inside Xero, the firm is able to work on the client's Xero file to ensure that whatever they prepare matches what the client sees in their own accounting software.

The other major benefit with a shared ledger is that the client can ask a question or ask for accounting assistance at any time. the accountant is then able to log in and access the clients' file very quickly and help as necessary. Prior to this, the client had to send a USB copy of the MYOB file, the accountant would complete the request, then send the USB copy of the updated MYOB file back to the client. While the accountant was working on the file, the client could not continue using MYOB on their end because the 'current' working file was with the accountant. Super inefficient.

2. Built with business owners (not accountants) in mind

The other massive benefit of using Xero is the user interface is very intuitive with how it lays things out, the language it uses, and its overall simplicity. I first used MYOB when I was studying accounting in high school. Even then, the software felt archaic, and it was difficult to find what you needed to work on. Saying that, once you had the time and patience to work it out, it was actually quite a powerful bit of software.

I just don't think the average business owner would be up to getting right into MYOB — and Xero is a much more welcoming interface. Not to mention easier to use without accounting experience.

3. You can use it anywhere, anytime

This is a follow-on from the first point here, but another major benefit of a cloud accounting software is that you can access your accounting software from pretty much any computer in the world in any location without needing to take copies of your files with you (like you previously needed to do with MYOB).

While there may be security risks with using a random computer, you could jump on a plane to a foreign country with your phone and wallet and passport, of course. If you had internet and a computer to use, you could log on to Xero if you needed to.

### 4. HubDoc & Dext for processing data and keeping copies of receipts

Another big perk of using Xero is that it connects with a whole heap of add-ons, which can increase the efficiency of your accounting administration. One example of the add-ons available are receipt or tax invoice saving and data recognition apps. The big one for a while was Receipt Bank (now renamed Dext). Xero also purchased HubDoc, which does the same thing as Dext, and it is included in the Xero business subscriptions.

I must say when HubDoc was brought out, the user interface was not as intuitive as Dext, so a lot of businesses still use Dext even though they must pay for it separately to Xero.

This sort of app is so important because, for example, you could be at the shops and just take a photo of your receipt in the app — all of the data is then uploaded into Xero itself, and you can even train these apps to learn where to reconcile certain items.

Also, they both allow email invoices you receive for online purchases or suppliers that send you invoices through email to be just forwarded to an email account and the software picks it up from there. It then saves an electronic copy of your invoice or receipt inside the app, saves another copy inside Xero as an attachment, and you'll have your original receipt as well if you don't throw it out — great for keeping records.

### 5. Quoting, Invoicing

Another thing that's worth mentioning about Xero is their quoting and invoicing that is built into the software. It can be set up to look really professional with your custom branding on it, and we used this from very early on when we started Inspire. Other clients have used the quoting and invoicing tools, and it works really effectively: it's able to deliver documents via email so when you receive it, you can actually see the PDF attached in the email or click the link and see the invoice or quote online.

### 6. Online Payments

You can also integrate your Xero invoicing with payment gateways or merchant facilities such as PayPal, Stripe, and many others. Invoicing and online payments in Xero can be fantastic for smaller businesses that don't have other software for these functions — giving their clients a professional-looking outcome for invoicing and payments.

### 7. Reporting

The reporting in Xero is great. Not only is it a lot more user-friendly than the menus in other accounting software, the reports it provides are actually dynamic — for example, you can click on a number in the profit and loss, and it drills down in a new tab for what the actual transactions in that account were. It makes reviewing the reports super efficient from a management perspective. They've also overhauled their reporting recently, providing much more customisation available in your production of all your standard reports.

### 8. Payroll

I've got to say the payroll feature is easy. I've been using it since day 1 of Inspire natively in Xero, and it's done the job really well. There are add-ons you can integrate (one of those is TANDA) if you have more intricate timesheet or award payment requirements. In addition, it does Signal Touch Payroll (STP), which is a requirement now for the ATO — where on preparation of your pay run, you click a button and lodge the required report with the ATO.

The automatic super payments are also really helpful. Once you set up all your employees' superannuation details in Xero, for each quarter that superannuation is due to be paid, Xero makes it easy to go in and pay this.

### 9. Integrating it with your other software (CRM, Sales Software, etc)

All these new apps are great, but what about the already existing software you know and like? Well, I've got a massive library of add-ons from a whole heap of different categories that you can integrate with your Xero file. I've mentioned payment gateways and receipt-keeping apps, but you can integrate them with your CRM, your email marketing software, Microsoft Office, Shopify, reporting apps (like Fathom), workflow systems (like ServiceM8 or WorkflowMax), and inventory management systems, such as Unleashed. There are heaps out there — you can see them all by going to https://apps.xero.com/au.

## What record-keeping do I need to consider for my business?

Now, let's address some common questions we get around record-keeping, especially from newer business owners.

### 1. How long do I need to keep records for?

The ATO advises that in most cases you need to hold onto your records for 5 years from the date that you lodge your tax return. So if you are lodging the 2022 financial year tax return, and you lodge that in May 2023, that is 5 years from May 2023 rather than 5 years from the end of the 2022 financial year.

If you have purchased an asset like a property or other asset that will attract capital gains tax upon the sale of it, you need to keep your records from the time that you purchased it through to five years after you lodged the tax return, which included its sale.

### 2. How can you store your records?

You can store your ATO related records either in paper or digital format. If your paper or digital format records are copies of an original document, they must be a true and clear copy of the original. It's also recommended that your digital copies are backed up. If you are using a receipt or invoice recognition software like Dext or HubDoc mentioned above, you will have a copy of your receipts in that software, plus a copy inside Xero — along with your original document if you keep that. Finally, your records should be in English unless the expense relates to expenses incurred outside of Australia.

## Best Practice Bookkeeping

I couldn't have a topic on financial rhythms without mentioning the importance best practices around bookkeeping. Here are some of the most common bookkeeping mistakes we see at Inspire, along with the suggested fix or best practice:

| Common Problem | What you can do about it? |
|---|---|
| DIY Bookkeeping<br><br><br><br>This one is common more so with newer business owners because they're looking to keep their ongoing costs down. But in a way, they are going to more likely shoot themselves in the foot. | Outsource your bookkeeping immediately! (If you don't already.) |

Unless you're a trained bookkeeper, you will likely not do an acceptable job, potentially leading to additional accounting fees to fix up the mistakes later, or it also could lead to under claiming or overclaiming expenses.

You also need to consider the opportunity cost of you doing your bookkeeping — for every hour of bookkeeping you do (likely not well), how much could you otherwise be earning working on client-related activities?

## Irregular Bookkeeping

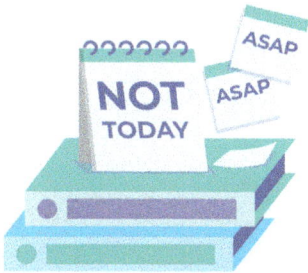

Another common problem I see is irregular bookkeeping. I made this mistake early in Inspire when things were busy, and I was wearing too many hats.

Set a frequent rhythm — weekly is ideal — where your bookkeeper works on your Xero file.

If you don't want to do weekly, then fortnightly is the next best option — otherwise monthly bookkeeping is the absolute max.

Basically, I would do the bookkeeping when the BAS was due, when I was getting chased by the ATO to lodge a BAS or a tax return.

The big problem here is not necessarily your struggle to get your lodgements done on time, but your inability to run your business and to make suitable decisions based on your recent financial performance (if your recent financial performance hasn't been bookkept yet).

## Not Enough Detail

When I refer to not enough detail, what I mean is that not enough time and thought was put towards how your reporting is laid out. The chart of accounts is the bookkeeping backbone to your reporting.

Spend time considering what your chart of accounts should look like with your bookkeeper or accountant.

It lists out all your different account types and account names. This needs a lot of detail to be able to bring your reports to life.

For instance, if you look at your profit and loss, and only see one line for subscription expenses, that's not going to mean too much as you see that fluctuate month to month. The best approach here is to break down your profit and loss statement into as many different expense categories as you can, even if it's to the point of having each supplier having their own line as a subcategory within an expense.

As an example, you could have Subscriptions: Office 365 suite; Subscriptions: Xero, and so on.

If you put this amount of work and detail in, your reports, such as your profit loss statement and your balance sheet, are going to look a lot more relevant and are easier to read. You're sometimes able to see trends even if you don't have this amount of detail.

Be sure that your bookkeeper uses these accounts as they should be used. This needs constant review and updating as your business changes and adds different expenses.

## Low Budget

Another mistake is that business owners don't put enough budget towards bookkeeping because they feel it's not a high-value activity.
I firmly believe it's actually more important than accounting because if your bookkeeping is not correct, then your accounting will not be correct.

You will also not be able to run your business and make wise financial decisions by looking at your accounting reports.

It might be a surprise, but a lot of our clients' bookkeeping expenses are more than their annual ordinary accounting expenses. This is because of the amount of time, effort, and energy that is required, and it's needed a lot more regularly than accounting advice throughout the year.

Make sure you see bookkeeping as a high-value activity.

Ask your accountant for feedback around your bookkeeper's quality of work for the price you're paying, and if the quality is too low, please consider finding a better quality (and likely more expensive) bookkeeper.

## No Review

The final common mistake I see with bookkeeping is that the business owner doesn't review what the bookkeeper has prepared.

The BAS gets lodged, and the tax returns were prepared, but the business owner didn't really look into the detail to review and to make sure it aligns with what they feel their experience was throughout that quarter or year.

Now your reaction might be to say, "Well, that's why I'm paying these people." But at the end of the day, they didn't have your experience or knowledge of the business: usually advisers see only a fraction of the context of these.

Make sure you are reviewing what your bookkeeper does each month at a minimum — review the profit and loss statement in detail, as well as the changes in the balance sheet month to month. Make sure it aligns with what you understand happened throughout that month. This can take practice to be able to read them, so you may need help the first few times you do this.

| I often have to make minor tweaks and changes to our bookkeeping once it's been finished by our bookkeeper to make sure it aligns with what I feel happened, and also it may make me aware of some problems going on that I wasn't aware of. | |
| --- | --- |

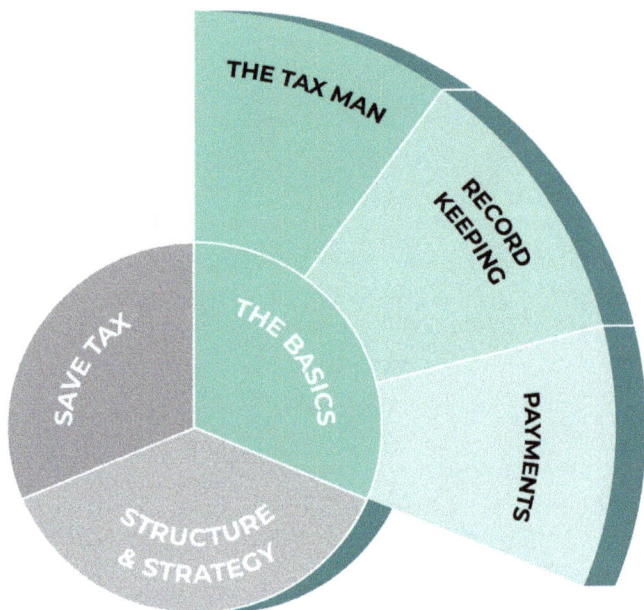

THE TAX MAN

RECORD
KEEPING

PAYMENTS

THE BASICS

SAVE TAX

STRUCTURE
& STRATEGY

# Chapter 3:
## Payments

*"Taxes, like tides, ebb and flow, but the savvy taxpayer knows when to make their payment to keep their financial ship afloat."*

**John Smith**

thought it would be helpful to include a chapter on payments of tax, planning for tax payments, and reducing tax debt if you have some accumulated. I have seen time and time again, especially with new or rapidly growing businesses, that tax payments catch them off guard.

Tax can be estimated and planned very well, and there are a number of things you can put in place to reduce the chance of getting caught with a surprise bill. In this chapter, I'll walk through some of the ways we do that for our clients at Inspire.

# Inspire's 3 Year Tax Forecaster

One of the tools we created at Inspire was the 3-year tax forecaster. This was borne out of a few incidents where we had clients frustrated that they didn't see bills coming due to the complexity of taxes with business ownership.

In the screenshot below, you'll see an example forecaster.

There are a few features to this forecaster which make it comprehensive and great to use to plan your cashflow for tax.

## *All your entities and each of their tax types*

It's important to consider all of the individuals and entities in your family group. Each entity will have its own tax considerations and types. You'll see in the forecaster that each entity is listed down the left side. Under each entity, you'll see that entity's corresponding tax types it is responsible for. For instance, a trading trust has a BAS, and that has both GST and PAYG withholding from wages.

## Current tax debt

The first thing to include is any existing tax debt. In the screenshot, there are no payment plans showing, otherwise there would be a monthly amount continuing until the payment plan was finished. The importance of showing any existing tax debt and payment plans is that the agreed terms need to be met, as well as any new additional debt for that entity.

## Future estimated obligations

Given this is a 3-year forecaster, we don't know with absolute certainty what all our obligations will be in this time period. We can base estimates of what has happened in the past or what the family group currently pays for certain taxes or obligations.

The reason I like the idea of going 3 years into the future is to account for significant changes to the rhythm of what is paid and when. This could happen for new business owners or businesses that are growing or shrinking — basically any change will likely change the tax payments owed by a family group.

## Account for a tax holiday

A tax holiday for new business owners is where the ATO doesn't know that an entity is earning untaxed income. Business income for the first financial year of earning is assessed when you lodge the first tax return with that business income included. The ATO will now know you're earning untaxed income, and if it's high enough, they will send you PAYG instalment notices for the following financial year, assuming that you will continue earning that same amount of untaxed income.

What will happen is your first full year of income tax on your untaxed income will be payable roughly the same time as your first few instalments for the next financial year — which, if unplanned, may result in a large tax bill from left field.

If you're aware of this tax holiday for business owners, you can account for it by setting up a separate bank account and regularly transferring an estimate of what you'll need into that account.

## Keep it continuously updated

Another key feature that you want in a tax forecaster is for it to be kept up to date.

You'll see in this example that there is black text and red text. The black text shows actuals or amounts for things paid in the past. The red is showing the expected or estimated obligation in the future.

As incomes are known and BAS quarters end, we're able to update for changes in the business and how this may affect monthly, quarterly, or annual tax payments. For example, if the business was growing and it was having an increase in the GST payable each quarter, we could reflect that on the forecaster into the future.

Similarly, if we know the outcome of a tax return, the ATO provides a way of calculating what the next year's PAYG instalments might be, and we can incorporate this into the tax forecaster. Given these reasons, the forecaster can be updated each time there is a confirmed obligation or if there is information that enables us to predict future amounts owing more accurately.

## Keeping tax aside for tax payments

The next thing that helps preparedness is to start keeping some money aside for tax payments. I would recommend using your tax forecaster to work out how much money you'll need to transfer into a separate bank account each week to make sure all your obligations are met. Having a consistent weekly amount going out of your business bank account is much more manageable than finding a massive amount when, say, a big BAS is due. It puts a smaller, consistent strain on your cashflow.

Also, when setting up this separate bank account I suggest that you hide it on your internet banking or set it up at a separate bank so that you don't see the balance often. This will remove temptation to raid the tax account for other things. So if you've got this account set up and are transferring money into it regularly, you should easily see if you're on track or not of your upcoming obligations.

To keep things simple, I use a single bank account for my whole family group's tax obligations to save the need for having a heap of tax savings accounts all over the place. The bookkeeping just needs to be on point if this is something you're keen to do. For example, if you look at your forecaster and you have roughly $20,000 a month owing in various taxes, you could work out how much to allocate each week by the following formula: 20,000 x 12 months / 52 weeks = weekly amount of $4,615.

## Quarterly Superannuation Payments

Another payment type that can catch us off-guard that isn't technically tax but is generally large and irregular is superannuation payments. This idea could apply to your quarterly employee's superannuation guarantee amount, or if you contribute to your fund once a year before 30th June, you may want to incorporate saving for that into this strategy, too.

What I would recommend is using either your tax account or another separate account to transfer a weekly amount to ensuring by the due date you've got the full amount set aside. For example, if you pay around about $25,000 every quarter for super, then, ideally, you've got around $1,925 going into this account each week ($25,000 x 4 quarters in a year divided by 52 weeks in a year).

## Payment Plans with the ATO

If you catch yourself in a bind and you become in debt with the ATO, then it's best to understand how they operate when it comes to paying it off over time. In my time as an accountant, I've always viewed the ATO as very reasonable when it comes to collecting debts from taxpayers — apart from in very limited circumstances where the taxpayer was rude, ignored them, and disregarded notices — they've been very helpful and understanding.

In terms of setting up a payment plan, what you'll need and the outcome to expect does depend on several things:

- How much the debt is (this will determine what team it goes to, as well as what level of approval)

- The taxpayer's history with the ATO (good lodgement and payment history will bode well. Constant problems will make them more hesitant to agree)

- The time you are requesting (the longer the request, the harder it will be)

- How much you can afford upfront

The ATO will also likely never grant a payment plan unless all lodgements for that entity are up to date. The information required to set one up will vary from nothing, right up to declaring any and all income, expenses, assets and liabilities of the entity to the ATO.

You'll find it easy to get a payment plan if:

- You have money to pay a figure upfront (they'll usually ask for between 20 and 25% of the debt upfront if you have it).

- Your repayment plan is under a year (even 2 or 3 years isn't unheard of — much more than this and it would need to be special circumstances).

- You have a good lodgement and payment history.

- You've got the ability to pay future debts as and when they are due.

It's important noting that if you default on your payment plan (miss a payment or miss a lodgement on time), your payment plan will usually be cancelled, and the full amount of your debt will show as overdue. If this happens to you, I'd recommend getting in touch with the ATO directly or via your tax agent / accountant to get a payment plan back in place.

## The ATO's Debt Recovery Process

The ATO, as I said earlier, are quite fair. One thing where I've seen people go wrong is ignoring the ATO's early intervention strategies, such as reminders or notices to lodge or pay. These letters will start in a friendly tone, but afterwards, they will start proceeding up a ladder of intensity and bad outcomes if that current letter is ignored.

## Director Penalty Notices

Things such as letter of demands and Director Penalty Notices (DPNs) are not nice ones to receive. These have fairly bad consequences; however, they won't send these out first. If you receive a DPN as a director of a business, this will mean the debt that your entity has failed to pay will soon be personally liable to you as the director. You need to immediately act on this, and if there is no action within 21 days, the amounts become recoverable from the director.

Your choices within that 21 days are to:

- Pay the debt or arrange a payment plan that the ATO accepts;

- Put the entity into voluntary administration;

- Put the entity into liquidation;

- Appoint a small business restructuring practitioner.

If paying the debt or a payment plan isn't accepted, I'd recommend speaking with an insolvency specialist as soon as is practical to advise you on this.

I hope Part 1 has given you the foundation knowledge to be able to manage your obligations with the ATO and ASIC. In the following Parts, we'll add to that knowledge with some often misunderstood but powerful strategies that will help you on your business journey.

# PART 2: Structure & Strategy

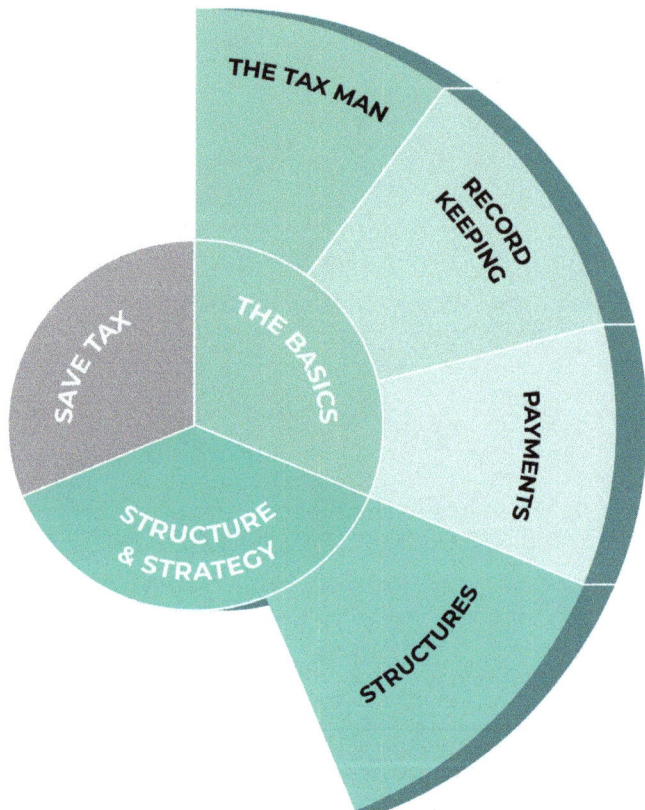

SAVE TAX

THE BASICS

STRUCTURE & STRATEGY

THE TAX MAN

RECORD KEEPING

PAYMENTS

STRUCTURES

# Chapter 4:
## Structures

*"Choosing a business structure is like picking a costume for a party; some folks go as a sleek corporation, while others prefer the trusty 'trust' outfit. Let's explore the costume closet of business!"*

**Anonymous**

In the coming chapter, I'm going to be sharing details on business structures. With business structures, it's important that these are set up correctly so that they give your business the best position from an asset protection and tax planning perspective.

Your business traction needs may change as your business grows, and it's important to regularly review and check that your structures are correct for your business and family group. Make sure you're working with an accountant who understands these structures in detail because if they don't, this step alone could cost thousands, tens of thousands, or even personal assets, such as the family home.

## 4 types of structures (tax rates, tax planning opportunity, asset protection)

| | INDIVIDUAL | COMPANY | TRUST | SMSF |
|---|---|---|---|---|
| **TAX RATES** | **47%** | 30%  25% | **0%** | 15%  0% |
| **TAX PLANNING** | ✗ | ✓ | ✓ | ✓✓ |
| **ASSET PROTECTION** | ✗ | ✓* | ✓* | ✓✓ |

We use the above diagram a lot to communicate about the different structure types with our clients at Inspire. You'll see across the top that we have 4 business structure options in Australia, and these also apply to investments as well — I will go into the detail on each shortly and also discuss when you might use a structure for business versus investment, along with why you would use one structure over another.

Down the left-hand side in the row headings, I've got a couple of different things to compare with the structures there. In the first row, you have the tax rate you might see in each of those structures; the ability for tax planning is in the second row; and in the third row is their ability to protect assets or their asset protection.

## Sole Trader

Let's start with sole trader in the first column. This is intentionally in red because we don't recommend our clients trade as a sole trader for their business. I've also put partnerships of individuals in the same bucket as sole trader — although they are slightly riskier because you are responsible for your other partners' decisions.

There are a number of reasons for us disliking people running a business as a sole trader, the first being the tax rate of up to 47% tax. This includes the 2% Medicare levy which all Australian resident individual taxpayers pay, however there are reductions for low-income earners for this.

Technically it is possible to pay more than 47% tax if you have a HECS / HELP debt, where this would be an additional 10% on top of your income if you're in the top bracket. If you don't have private hospital cover, you will also pay an additional Medicare levy surcharge if you make the income level, and that is an additional up to 1.5% of your income. My calculation suggests that the top tax rate that an individual could get to is as much as 58.5% in tax (that's more than half of their generated income goes straight to the tax man). However, for simplicity, the table will say up to 47% tax as a sole trader.

When you're tax planning as a sole trader, there aren't as many strategies to save tax because you are earning your income in your own name, without the ability to share income amongst your family group. Once income is earned in your sole trader name, it cannot be allocated to other family members or entities for them to pay their tax at their respective rates. This is the key limitation from a tax planning perspective of being a sole trader. If you run a business as a sole trader, you still do have the ability to use small business tax planning rules like you would under most of the other structures.

When it comes to asset protection as a sole trader, there is very little protection. This is because the legal entity running your business is you as an individual, and any assets you own as an individual (or jointly with other people) are technically assets of that same entity that run the business. So, in the case that you are sued or need to pay creditors, those personal or investment assets held in your own name could be used to pay out. I will share more on asset protection in Chapter 5.

## Company

Moving on to the company structure, you will notice that my colours in the graph change from a red to a green colour. This is because companies are something that we use at Inspire regularly, along with trusts, and sometimes in that far right column, structuring with SMSFs (self-managed super funds).

In terms of the tax rate of a company, there are actually 2 tax rates and that depends on the turnover and the type of activities that the company runs. The first tax rate is 25% and that is for companies who run businesses and have a turnover of less than $50 million. The second tax rate is 30% and that is for businesses who turn over more than $50 million, or companies where the activities are predominantly investment activities.

If you have a company that invests and runs a business, the passive income that company receives cannot exceed 80% of the total income for the company to pay that reduced tax rate of 25%. (We wouldn't recommend this anyway because we don't want trading entities with large amounts of investment assets.)

When it comes to tax planning and companies, companies actually have a reasonable amount of their ability to tax plan assuming that they are set up well. In addition to the normal business tax planning strategies, companies can pay dividends to shareholders or salaries to related family members (ensuring that they are at a market rate to be seen as legal). This allows income of the company to be paid to other working family members or shareholders of the company. I will go into more detail about getting money out of companies and trusts shortly.

When it comes to asset protection, companies offer good protection if they are set up well. There will be more on asset protection in chapter 5, but for now the key with companies is that they are seen as separate legal entities compared to the directors who run the company. This means that if the company is sued, at a high level, the company's assets are exposed but not the personal assets of the directors (there are ways that this can be sidestepped so it is not bullet-proof — again, more in Chapter 5).

## Trusts

When I refer to trusts in this table, I'm predominantly referring to discretionary trusts or trusts sometimes referred to as family trusts.

Just a side note on unit trusts — a unit trust is where there is usually a fixed interest in the trust that is allocated or split up by the unitholders. Unitholders can have ownership of the income rights or the capital rights of the trust (or both), and when we look at the tax outcome, including tax planning for unit trusts, we need to look at who owns the units in that unit trust (which would hopefully be a discretionary trust anyway), although sometimes they have been set up with individual unitholders. But assuming they are discretionary trusts, we can follow the commentary in this section around trusts, even if you have a unit trust as your business entity.

In the table you will see that trusts have a 0% tax rate. What I'm not saying here is that if you structure as a trust, then you won't pay any income tax. Rather with trusts, they give or allocate their profit in the year to other people or entities in the family group, and then those people or entities pay the tax on their share of the profits allocated to them. We call these people or entities the beneficiaries of the trust.

In terms of tax planning and trusts, trusts are currently the most flexible of all the entities when it comes to allocating income within the family group. To be a beneficiary of the trust, you must fall within the definition of a beneficiary per the trust's deed, which are the rules set out for that trust that was set up when it was created. This is ordinarily set up with the key family members as primary beneficiaries.

Secondary beneficiaries that are normally included in the trust deed are not necessarily named beneficiaries, but rather referred to as the primary beneficiaries' spouse, children, grandchildren, parents, grandparents, aunts, uncles, in-laws, and so on. You will need to make sure you read and understand your trust deed to make sure the people you are wanting to allocate your trusts profit to are able to receive that per the trust deed. So if someone you want to distribute profit of the trust to is a beneficiary, then you can allocate that profit from the trust and then that person or entity pays the tax on their share of profit.

There are a couple of exemptions based on industry or type of income that a trust receives that may limit its ability to freely allocate income within a family group, but generally you are able to allocate the profit from a trust within a family group as you see fit, without the need for it to be seen as market value (like a salary mentioned above in the company section).

So from a tax planning perspective, trusts are great. And when it comes to asset protection, trusts also enjoy the same benefits of companies if they have been set up well.

A trust is not seen as a separate legal entity on its own and needs a role in the trust called a trustee. The trustee makes the day-to-day decisions on behalf of the trust. A trustee can be an individual or a company. You can have more than 1 trustee of a single trust, although this is rare.

The relationship I usually compare to trustee and trust is that the trustee is a legal entity, like an adult would be looking after a child, and in Australia, the child is not seen as a legal entity until they are 18 years old. At minimum, a trust that runs a business should be set up with a company as its trustee rather than an individual because of the separation between that company and the individual.

# How to take the money out of each structure

One very common question we get asked by clients is, "How do you take the money out of each company or trust?"

## *Company*

### 1. Salary

The first way to take money out of a company is by paying the business owner, or you, a salary. This is a pretty relatable method for paying yourself from a structure, even for newer business owners, because pretty much everyone would have some form of employment income in their lifetime — and it is basically your own structure paying you a salary. If you pay yourself a salary as a business owner, you now need to process this salary through single touch payroll, the same way you would for any of your other employees.

It also means you need to take tax out from the gross payments, PAYGW, or Pay As You Go Withholding. It also means you need to pay superannuation on top of your own salary too.

The current superannuation rates as at the time of publishing are:

| Financial Year | Rate |
|---|---|
| 2024 (1 July 2023 to 30 June 2024) | 11.00% |
| 2025 (1 July 2024 to 30 June 2025) | 11.50% |
| 2026 (1 July 2025 to 30 June 2026) | 12% |

Please note that these superannuation rates have changed several times over the years, so if you are making decisions based off this, just double-check that these rates are still current. The good news is that if you use Xero as your payroll system, your tax withholding and superannuation is automatically calculated by the software.

### 2. Loan (Division 7A)

The second way to take money out of a company is through paying the business owners a loan. This is where you would literally transfer money from the company's bank account to your personal (or another related entity's bank account), and we treat that as a loan from the company to the entity receiving the money.

There are specific tax rules that govern what happens when you loan money from companies, and that section of law is called Division 7A. In short, there are minimum repayments to be made each year and interest to be paid at an ATO dictated rate, otherwise you will end up with adverse (and expensive) tax outcomes.

If you've had a company for a while and have been working with an accountant, you may have run into these rules before as well as what we call director's loans or Division 7A loans when we work with clients. They're not necessarily a bad thing or something to be avoided at all costs, but they are definitely something that needs monitoring and managing, especially if they are increasing year on year.

I go into much more detail into Division 7A and the many solutions for it in Chapter 9.

### 3. Dividend

The third way to take money out of a company is through paying a dividend.

Dividends are paid to the shareholders (also known as the members or owners of a company). This means it's incredibly important when setting up a company to consider who your shareholders need to be — not only for asset protection (more on that shortly), but it's definitely very important for tax purposes.

We need to make sure the shareholder of the company is in a position to receive dividends from a tax perspective - not just when we set the structure up, but also in the future. We're often not certain how that looks, so we need to make sure our options for tax are flexible.

I give examples of what the shareholders should be in Chapter 6 when we talk about growth in relation to your business structures.

## Trust

### 1. Salary

The first way to take money out of a trust is to pay a salary. This works the same way as paying a salary from a company, but you are paying a salary from your trust instead. You need to pay superannuation on top of your payments and also take withholding tax from your gross payments — just the same as you would a company mentioned above.

When it comes to trusts and taking salaries, there are often more flexible ways to take money out of a trust for the business owner. These would be using a combination of drawings and distributions (see points 2 and 3 below).

### 2. Loan (Drawings)

The second way to take money out of a trust is to loan the money from the trust, which we often call drawings. Drawings do not have the same rules as Division 7A loans from companies. There are no minimum repayments or interest required to be paid.

If you draw money out of a trust as a loan, we record this on the balance sheet as drawings or a lone, and it often gets netted off against the third way to take money out of a trust — distributions.

### 3. Distributions

The third way to take money from a trust is called distributions, which are paid to people we call 'beneficiaries' of the trust. The distribution process is the allocation of the profit that the trust makes each year, and the process of allocating these distributions needs to be done before 30th June every financial year for the financial year that it relates to.

For instance, if a trust makes $100,000 of profit in the 2023 financial year (before 30th June 2023), the trustees need to decide and document which beneficiaries receive this money. It's useful to think of dividends in companies as payments of the prior year's profit, while distributions are trusts payments from the current year profit.

In Chapter 7, I share more detail on who and what normally qualify as beneficiaries, with the pros and cons for distributing to each.

## SMSFs – Self-Managed Super Funds

When it comes to structuring with self-managed super funds, we don't structure the business in the SMSF itself, but rather the ownership of a company or trust could be within an SMSF. There are many rules relating to this, so please don't do this without advice or assume there are no limitations in what you can do with ownership of businesses within your SMSF if you have one.

In terms of the tax rates of superannuation, the rate is either at 15% or 0% depending on the status of the members' balance in the fund. The 15% tax rate applies to a member's balance that is in accumulation mode. This is generally when members are accumulating superannuation throughout their life and are not receiving a pension from their super fund on that portion of their balance.

The 0% tax rate applies to members who are in pension mode and have met a condition of release that means their superannuation is tax-free on its earnings. The current rules are the member needs to have either reached the age of 65 or the member has reached the age of 60 and has ceased gainful employment (you retire or quit a job) for your superannuation balance to possibly be seen as this pension-eligible tax rate of 0%.

Again, there are a heap of rules that go with this and you must make sure to get advice around your specific circumstances before making any decisions on your structuring or other financial matters. I've also got to highlight that this 0% tax rate is pretty impressive because you don't even need to live in a tax haven to achieve a 0% tax on your earnings.

There is a limitation to this that was brought in for the 2018 financial year which limits the portion of your super fund that can be taxed at 0%. This limit is subject to change each financial year and is started at $1.6 million. It is currently at $1.9 million, which means the earnings you receive from up to $1.9 million of your superannuation balance can be taxed at 0%. If you were to have more than this amount in super, you would pay 15% tax on the earnings above this amount.

Please note that this is a per person amount, rather than a per family group amount, so if you have a spouse, your combined limit is $3.8 million. Keep in mind that this is tested on a per person basis, so you can't have 1 spouse with $3 million in their super, and another spouse with $0.8 million in their super and receive all the income tax-free.

When I talk about an SMSF's ability to tax plan, the thing I just can't get past is the low tax environment of 15% or 0% tax. Now, there are some instances where you won't be able to access the money that's earned in super, and that is generally for people in accumulation mode under the age of 60 who have been accumulating their balance throughout their life. But you'll see in the table below the comparison of compounding investments at different tax rates, and you'll be surprised at what a 15% or 0% tax rate does.

And lastly, when it comes to asset protection and SMSFs, they are the best structure for asset protection. This is because superannuation has protection even through bankruptcy of a person, so their superannuation balance cannot be attacked even if they are getting sued. This is limited, however, in the case of a person intentionally dumping a whole heap of money in superannuation, knowing something bad is going to happen in order to protect it. So I understand that in the case of you taking actions outside of what you would normally do, from a historical perspective, these transactions can be unwound.

# Advanced SMSF Topics

## Comparing the low tax environment of superannuation

One scenario I show clients when they're looking at what structure to invest money in is showing the difference in tax outcome. For example, where you look to invest in, let's say, a bucket company paying 30% tax versus a super fund in accumulation mode at 15% versus a super fund in pension mode paying 0% tax.

In the table below you can see those 3 options. What the calculation aims to do is show the difference if you were to invest $55,000 a year ($27,500 for 2 people) as an annual contribution to your investment pool that earns an 8% investment return each year. In each scenario there is also a starting balance of $100,000.

The first thing each scenario does is reduce the annual contribution of $55,000 by the relevant tax rate — either 30% in a bucket company, which receives that initial contribution, or the super fund paying 15% on contributions tax as a concessional contribution for 2 people in the family group. Already in the super fund, you're saving 15% compared to the bucket company as the money goes in.

Next, model shows an 8% return on the annual balance reduced by the relevant income tax — again, 30% in the company versus 15% or 0% in the super fund. You

| Number of people | | | 2 |
|---|---|---|---|
| | | | |
| Annual Contribution pre tax | | | 55000 |
| Less 15% super contributions tax | | | -8250 |
| Money invested - SMSF net of 15% contributions tax | | | 46750 |
| Money invested if Bucket Company (assume 30% tax) | | | 38500 |
| | | | |
| | | | |
| Investment return | | | 8% |
| | | | |
| | | | |
| Option | Option 1 | Option 2 | Option 3 |
| Tax rate | 30% | 15% | 0% |
| How | Bucket company | Accumulation | Pension |
| | | | |
| Starting balance | $100,000 | $100,000 | $100,000 |
| Finanical year | | | |
| 2022 | $144,100 | $153,550 | $154,750 |
| 2023 | $190,670 | $210,741 | $213,880 |
| 2024 | $239,847 | $271,822 | $277,740 |
| 2025 | $291,779 | $337,056 | $346,710 |
| 2026 | $346,618 | $406,725 | $421,196 |
| 2027 | $404,529 | $481,133 | $501,642 |
| 2028 | $465,682 | $560,600 | $588,523 |
| 2029 | $530,261 | $645,471 | $682,355 |
| 2030 | $598,455 | $736,113 | $783,694 |
| 2031 | $670,469 | $832,918 | $893,139 |
| | | | |
| Net benefit vs bucket company | | $162,450 | $222,671 |

Not financial advice, assuming that the annual contribution doesn't earn investment income the year it is invested

can see at the 'Net benefit vs Bucket Company' row of the table that there is a substantial tax saving if you were to invest in a super fund in pension, but even in accumulation where after 10 years your saving is over $160,000 compared to investing in a bucket company.

This difference is even further exacerbated if your fund is in pension mode at 0% tax. Please note, even in pension mode you will still pay 15% tax if you do a concessional contribution in this case as I have modelled a pre-tax contribution of $55,000, say from business profits. The difference between the accumulation in pension result is only the tax on the 8% return each year — it still adds up to be a considerable amount.

## 8 Benefits of a Self-Managed Super Fund

I have had a love for SMSFs ever since I first started in accounting. SMSF is an acronym that stands for a **Self-Managed Superannuation Fund**. It is an option for you to directly manage your own superannuation through your own entity that you set up and are the trustee of. The alternative is to be a member of an industry or corporate super fund where the management of your superannuation is delegated to a business along with a pool of other people's superannuation money.

In my first year of working in accounting, when I was straight out of school, I was auditing SMSFs at KPMG and learning about the rules of SMSFs. In 2010, when I changed employers, I went from auditing dozens of funds every year to preparing the tax compliance and administration for every fund that the firm looked after. In 2011, I set up a self-managed super fund with my parents which gave me hands-on experience as a member of a fund. It taught me the complexities involved when preparing investment strategies, even transactions like my parents taking pensions from the fund as well.

I saw everything from basic, simple funds that were invested in shares and cash, right through to some crazy investments in famous porn posters (you read that right — very strange), and even a fund where the member had sold a business, paid a huge chunk of cash into his fund, and had been living out of his fund to put food on the table and pay his mortgage. Oh dear!

Around about 28% of our clients at Inspire have an SMSF and I have advised hundreds of trustees over the years in things such as:

- Carrying out property development
- Fund businesses
- Investing in private companies
- Angel investing
- Purchasing commercial property
- Purchasing residential property
- Borrowing money from banks
- Borrowing money from related parties
- Paying no tax on massive capital gains

— all using self-managed super funds.

On a national level, there were about 70 SMSFs set up every single day in 2021, and I feel more Australians are seeing the benefits and freedoms that SMSFs give. On 30th June 2021, there were 597,900 SMSFs in Australia, with 1,114,529 members — that's about 1 in every 23 Australians.

There are plenty of reasons why we love them at Inspire, which we'll explore in this chapter. Eight of the main benefits are:

1. Engagement with your super

2. Family fund

3. Control tax

4. Investment strategy

5. Leverage

6. Insurance

7. Incapacity planning

8. Estate planning

## Engagement With Your Super

### The difference between SMSF v corporate super funds

One of the first things I talk about when discussing engagement with a client is the differences between a self-managed super fund versus their current corporate or industry super fund. The first thing here is that one of the differences is in the name. The industry or corporate super fund will manage your super for you, whereas you need to manage your SMSF yourself.

Another thing that we find with members of SMSFs is that they are more engaged with how much super they have, how much it is earning, where it is invested, and what their targets or goals are with it. We often see them involving their SMSF in their business if they run a business, for instance, by buying a commercial property that their business rents from their SMSF. I strongly believe that self-managing your super gives you a much stronger connection to your super and your overall wealth creation journey.

## Comparing the costs

The other question that I am often asked by clients is, "What are the differences in costs for running an SMSF versus a corporate or industry super fund?" An industry or corporate super fund generally charges a percentage-based fee on the balance of your superannuation, while an SMSF usually has fixed administration and compliance costs associated with it.

**Break Even**

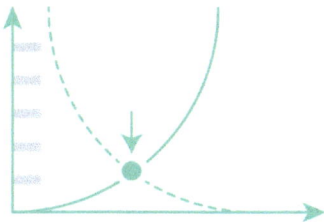

There will be a break-even point. To work that out, you'll need to have a look at the current fees that you're paying in your industry super fund and compare that with the relatively fixed costs of running your SMSF.

For instance, if you are paying 1.5% in total fees and have a balance of $200,000 in your super, then you will be paying $3,000 in fees each year. This is compared to say an SMSF, where the total running costs of your SMSF might be priced at $3,000, while your balance is anywhere up to $500,000. If these are your numbers, then your break-even point for the SMSF is $200,000. (Note: this excludes setup costs for the SMSF, which can be a few thousand in any case.)

Regardless, costs are only one thing to consider when setting up an SMSF and are usually not a top priority for clients. It is the other outcomes that you can achieve with your super fund that make the decision to switch to a SMSF a no-brainer.

## How much do you need in super to set one up?

One of the most popular questions when it comes to SMSFs is, "How much do I need to set one up?" If you were to Google this question, then the most common answer that would pop up is anywhere between $200,000 and $250,000. Now, keep in mind that this is usually referring to the fund as a total, rather than each member on their own. So, if you have a husband and wife with $125,000 each in super, that would combine together to give a $250,000 fund.

The cost of setting up an SMSF is usually the main factor to consider its suitability for your situation (which we've gone into a bit of detail in the previous section) — the break-even point of fees is usually the discussion. My opinion is that setup costs aren't the be all and end all of an SMSF, and while I would strongly question why someone would set up a fund with $50,000 in their super, there is no legal minimum you need to set one up. I believe that there are other benefits people can enjoy with SMSFs, and the costs are secondary considerations. These benefits are usually related to what you can do in SMSFs compared with the limitations of other industry funds, such as:

- To invest in direct residential or commercial property

- To loan money for the purchase of certain investments (most commonly, for residential and commercial property)

- To access non-listed investments

- To invest in physical holdings of precious metals

- The ability for the SMSF to pay for learning in conferences around superannuation for the trustees

- The ability to pool money with other non-related super funds to make large investments in businesses or property development

- Not having to lodge a form with a third-party super provider (for whatever reason) and wait days or weeks for a response

- Flexibility in how and when you draw your pension throughout the year

- A combination of any of the above, and more!

At the end of the day, I feel the question of how much you need in super to warrant an SMSF is highly dependent on what your intentions are to do with it, and the cost should be considered relative to those intentions.

### The "SM" in SMSF

I just wanted to pop in a final reminder and a bit of a warning that the "SM" in SMSF means self-managed. This means that it requires your own personal diligence to set up and run the fund. It has compliance requirements and rules of the game that you need to abide by so that you don't breach the superannuation rules, which can have quite large penalties if broken. There is also an annual audit required by a third-party auditor which, as accountants, we can organise on your behalf. Their role is to make sure that you haven't breached the Superannuation Act and that your reports are accurate.

If you are working with a good accountant, then this process is easy and staying within the rules is as simple as asking a question when one pops up. I have seen quite a few sticky situations where the trustees have knowingly or unknowingly breached the rules or had questionable advice, and we've had to dig them back out of a hole. The best thing to do is work with someone who knows the boundaries from the start and who helps you work within them while leveraging the power of an SMSF.

## Leverage

The next benefit to run through is the ability for an SMSF to borrow money and leverage their own cash position.

An SMSF cannot borrow money directly in its own right, but it

# LRBA - Limited Recourse Borrowing Arrangement

SMSF cannot borrow to buy property directly

Bare Trust sits in the middle as a "shadow" purchasing entity
- can be borrowed from a bank
- can be you own cash (bucket company)

uses a bare trust to sit in between the SMSF and the asset it is purchasing. We call these special requirements for lending to SMSF's limited recourse borrowing arrangements (LRBAs). Cash can be borrowed from a bank, which is the most common, but money can also be borrowed from your own entities (such as a bucket company) to purchase an asset.

**OUTSIDE SUPER**
- Slightly less complex lending
- Higher tax outcome
- Business/personal income to service. Can adjust for existing rent if you will owner occupy
- Can use other security for deposit

**VS**

**BOTH**
- Can owner occupy
- Can see LVR's go to 80%

**INSIDE SUPER** (SMSF)
- "LRBA"
- Super contributions and rental income to service
- Tax 15% or 0$
- Very few lenders (Still good)
- Typically higher rate
- Lender can require advice (legal and financial planning)
- Needs cash deposit
- Cannot borrow for constructions costs unless off plan

In terms of the broad lending rules, one of the things that we usually do is show our clients the difference between what the normal environment looks like when lending outside super versus inside super. Some of the pros and cons can be seen in the table above, but one of the great things is that, usually, your borrowing capacity in your SMSF doesn't have to rely on any borrowing capacity outside of super.

In terms of the deposit required, there are some lenders who will lend 80% of your property value depending on the postcode and the asset type that you're buying, but it is common for most lenders in the space to lend at least 70% of most assets. That means that you will need to have between a 20% and 30% deposit, plus stamp duty, and, often, have a little bit of cash leftover in your fund after settlement to pay the bills and other expenses of the fund. Some lenders want to see about 10% of your property value in liquid cash after settlement.

At the end of the day, the details here depend on the property that you are looking to purchase and the lenders you are working with. My recommendation is to speak to a mortgage broker who has experience in SMSF lending and let them do the running around to match you to the best lender for what you're looking to do.

The other thing to keep in mind is that you can only borrow for 1 single asset. What this means is you can't purchase something like a house and land package where there are 2 separate contracts and you are funding the land purchase and the construction costs separately.

You can purchase an off-the-plan property from a developer where there is a single contract, though. You especially need to watch out for properties that have 2 titles such as commercial properties across two titles.

There are sometimes ways around this where you take out two loans, but this can prove a bit tricky when the goal is to meet the superannuation rules while also keeping in line with the lender's requirements.

Property is the most common asset that is purchased using lending in super. You can also borrow money to purchase other assets such as a single set of shares. Even though you are buying more than 1 share, if it's a single ASX listed share and you're buying a parcel of them, the rules are written so that this is considered a single acquirable asset.

So you could buy, as an example, 100 BHP shares as a parcel and have a loan on that. But if you were to take a loan out to purchase 50 BHP shares and 50 Rio Tinto shares under the same loan agreement, then that will not work for the single acquirable asset rule.

The other thing before we wrap up the leverage section is to mention that if you are borrowing money from your own entity like a bucket company, then the loan has to be on commercial terms. Please be careful with this and seek advice if this is what you are planning to do.

## Some Cool Things You Can Do With Your SMSF

### Buy commercial or residential property

An SMSF can be used to purchase a commercial or residential property:

When it comes to residential property, a member or a related person of a member cannot live in that property

**Residential**

**Commercial**

(ie owner occupy is not permitted). But, it's still a fantastic way to grow your superannuation balance by investing in high-quality residential property. You can also borrow money from banks, as I've mentioned earlier in this section. This can mean that if you've got a few hundred thousand dollars in super, you may be able to buy a fairly significant property with help from lenders.

In terms of commercial property though, a member's business or even a related party's business *can* rent a commercial property that's owned in that person's SMSF. So the difference is that the business can owner occupy the property as long as it is a commercial property. This means that you can use your SMSF in a way that may benefit your business by securing a commercial property, which helps both the long-term stability and growth of your business.

It means you are essentially both the tenant and the landlord, where your business is the tenant and you are the landlord through your own SMSF. While that may be the case, there are requirements for you to make sure that the rent is market rate, and this should be confirmed or documented where the auditor of your fund also checks this.

## Become your own bank

Another thing you can do with your SMSF is to lend to other people or entities. There are restrictions on lending money to members themselves, but if you have a related party business, there is a way to lend up to 5% of the value of the total assets in the SMSF to that related party business. This is seen as an in-house asset and is heavily scrutinised by the auditor and reportable to the ATO in the tax return. As long as it's on market-rate terms and it does not exceed 5% of the total assets of the fund, there are not too many things that can unwind this.

A bit of a trap here is this: say that you've got $1,000,000 in your SMSF in value, most of which is invested in the stock market. If you were to lend $50,000 to a related party business, this would be exactly 5% of your total fund balance. If, in the next month, the share market lost 20% of its value, your $50,000 loan would now be worth 6.25% of the total value of the fund, therefore breaching the in-house asset rules.

Because of this, we often caution people who are looking to explore this option with the example above, and we make sure they are constantly monitoring what is happening with the total value of the fund if they are close to lending the 5% maximum.

The other alternative is that you can lend money to a non-related party and this is not seen as an in-house asset.

An example of how people have used this in the past is by lending a friend money to start their business or fund growth in their business. As with most things regarding SMSFs, care needs to be taken to make sure everything is done carefully and at market-rate value.

The interest rate relative to what the loan is for, relative to the security taken, the term provided, and the repayment terms are all very important and must be right. This is extremely high-risk, especially if there is limited security taken for the loan. Risk and diversification need to be considered in the investment strategy for the fund.

In summary, I wouldn't ever recommend people set up an SMSF to loan money out (nor am I able to advise from a financial planning perspective on what an SMSF should invest in) – but an SMSF *can* do these things, assuming that the right documentation is put in place.

## Invest in private companies or trusts

Another thing that an SMSF can invest in is private companies or private unit trusts. There are some restrictions around this, where the SMSF or its related parties cannot have control through an ownership share of more than 50% — or even perceived control through influence on other parties, nor a tie-breaker ability (in the case of shareholders where shareholders disagree).

There must be a genuine inability to control the entity, but even an ownership share of 50% is possible. This being the case, if you have two or more business partners, you can technically set up companies or trusts with your super funds providing the start-up capital and then run a business that is owned by super.

Another example is starting up an investment entity where you have multiple families investing in a big project or investment, such as property development, a large property purchase, or an investment fund. Again, anything like this needs to be done with care and should always be done with the right advice.

## Develop property

Another thing that we see very commonly done with SMSFs is where a family group develops property. The cool thing about this is that there are many ways to structure a property development that incorporate your super balance.

A few years ago, I met a group of four potential business partners. They were looking to do a property development using money that each one had saved plus equity in their houses. The development size they were thinking about was around the $2 to $4 million mark. They all had some form of experience in developments larger than that $2 to $4 million range through their current and previous employment history, but they thought that they were limited in development size based solely on their available equity in savings.

One of those four people was a client of Inspire. The client organised a property development structuring session including all four of them, using us as advisers. By the end of that session, we were able to talk through how they could use their combined super balances to significantly increase their development equity position. In turn, this would allow them to access more funding and be able to do a larger development.

After that session, they have been hunting for larger developments, given the increased scope, and have recently begun the process on a $10 million development. This is much more than they thought they could access previously, all thanks to the power of using their super balance to assist. We've also seen situations where two unrelated family groups come together to fund a small development through super and even engage a related-party builder to complete the construction if there are houses to be built.

There are about half a dozen ways that we have structured this type of thing in the past where averaging superannuation opens up more options for either development size or cash flow. We have also created options around where the bulk of the profit goes, whether that is inside or outside of super.

Of course, all of these options are extremely complex, and I'm proud to say that our team have a bit of a speciality (and a genuine interest) in getting the most out of the situation for the maximum benefit of the client. So if you do want to talk more about this, we have options for running property development structuring sessions that incorporate super. Please reach out for a strategy call if this is something you are keen on exploring.

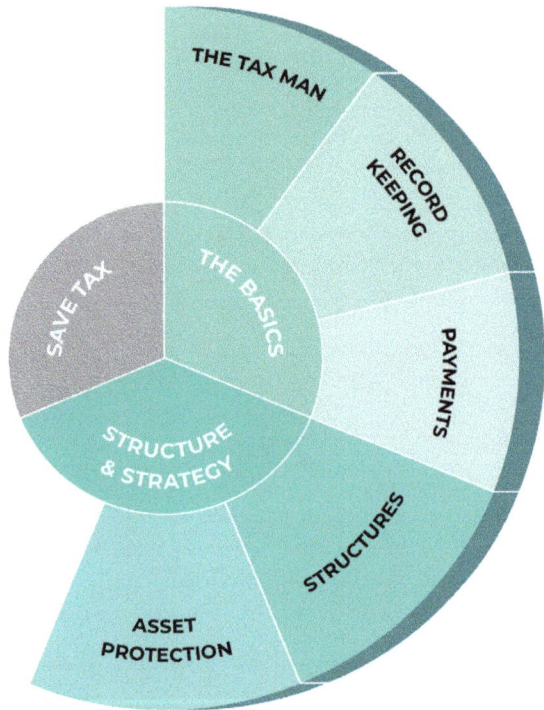

# Chapter 5:
## Asset Protection

*"Asset protection is like the secret handshake between your wealth and Murphy's Law – it's all about expecting the unexpected!"*

**William Davies**

Asset protection is something I feel people only take seriously when they need it, but, unfortunately, it doesn't work like that. You need asset protection measures set up almost from the very beginning — basically, as soon as your business kicks off. If you don't have the knowledge of what to do at the start, you need to implement these measures as soon as practically possible.

This is because many asset protection measures can be unwound if they are implemented within a certain timeframe from when you may have had a bankruptcy or liquidation event. Those are intense examples, but good asset protection will also make you less of a target — so much so that people might not even bother pursuing bankruptcy or forcing a liquidation due to the expense for the low or no reward on their end.

I will also mention that we are not lawyers and this is not legal advice. We recommend that with asset protection strategies, they should be reviewed and recommended in line with lawyers' recommendations.

## 4 types of risk

The first thing we'll go through is answering the question, "What are the sort of risks of running a business?" If you've never had any run-ins with getting sued or incurring massive amounts of debt, you may actually not see the importance of asset protection. So I want to share the things we should be concerned about first.

The other thing to remember is that there are insurances you can take out to cover some of these or reduce these risks, but that insurance should be a first line of defence. However, there are instances where you may not be insured or have money owing beyond what you were insured for, so I don't believe insurance is the way you totally remove your need for asset protection.

### Employees

The first group of people over you might be at risk from is the people that work for you. This may be frustrating to hear, but, unfortunately, employment law does not seem to be written with a balanced consideration to the employee and to the employer, but rather written in favour of the employee, and, in many situations, to the disadvantage of the employer.

I appreciate that strong protection for employees who are mistreated by their employer are needed, but I struggle with the concept that general businesses have to constantly cop tough laws instead of reasonably balanced laws. I also heard from a good friend and client who works in HR that WorkCover fines can be over $60,000 per breach — that's a crazy amount of money for breaching very convoluted laws. So we need to be aware of the risks around employees.

## Clients

The next category of risk I usually address is clients. You might end up getting sued by a client if you cause them loss or don't carry out what you agreed to in your contract with them. I feel this category varies greatly depending on the industry that you're in — you may be in a very low-risk industry for the client, therefore probably don't have to worry about this too much. But I feel industries like health or finance would need to be very mindful of this one.

## Suppliers

Suppliers are the next category of risk, and I classify suppliers anyone you pay money to, including, as an example, the ATO. This can pertain to your landlord as well, which is likely one of your biggest commitments and one of your most complex contracts if you have a lease. Suppliers, if they are unpaid, can force an entity into liquidation if you don't meet certain obligations and they pursue you.

## Competitors

The last category is competitors, and I feel this is pretty low-risk, but inadvertently using someone else's intellectual property or defaming someone else in the industry may end you up in hot water.

## Risk Spectrum

HIGH RISK                    LESS RISK

The other thing when I think about risk is I recognise someone's tolerance to risk is often different to the next person's. I've met clients who don't feel they need any asset protection at all, even after explaining the risks — but then other clients, who I perceive are in a very low-risk position, take asset protection very seriously and want all the things in place. Because of this, I usually describe what I call the Risk Spectrum.

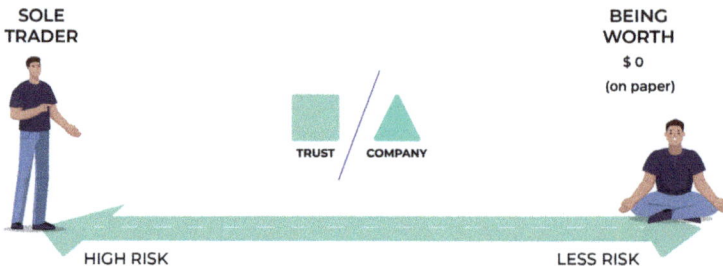

SOLE TRADER

BEING WORTH
$0
(on paper)

TRUST / COMPANY

HIGH RISK                    LESS RISK

It is a visual representation of the different levels of asset protection.

You'll see above on the far-left side is sole trader or person, which offers next to no asset protection. I mentioned earlier in the book that we don't recommend sole traders for a few reasons — definitely tax, but also asset protection.

Moving along the spectrum about halfway, you've got a rectangle and triangle sitting there, representing trust and company structures. So, it doesn't necessarily matter which way around your combination of structures are — more so that you have these things in place so that your business is a separate legal entity to you as a person.

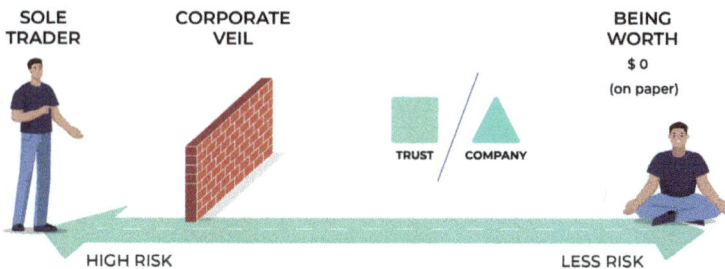

In the diagram, between the person and the company/ trust, you'll see a brick wall. This is a representation for the corporate veil — which is that separation where your company is a separate legal entity to you. In a way, that is a level of asset protection between your business and you as a person, with your personal assets. Unfortunately, there are ways the corporate veil can be pierced.

I talk about 3 main ways the veil can be peirced, those being:

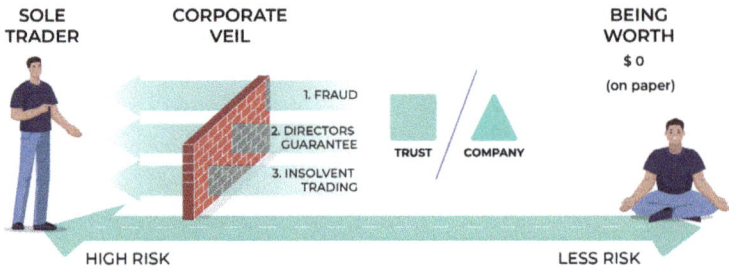

1. **Fraud** — if you commit fraud in your company, you've intentionally deceived people for your own gain. I actually do not have sympathy if the corporate veil is pierced under these circumstances.

2. **Director's Guarantees** — these are contractual agreements you might sign that basically says if the company doesn't pay a bill, then the director guarantees that they will pay for the bill from their own personal funds. These are very common on commercial leases and finance agreements with banks (even if the finance agreement is secured against a car). You could also find this on some suppliers' terms and conditions, so you need to be careful what you're signing — and understand if you are signing a guarantee, that means money needs to come out of your pocket in the event the company cannot pay it. The person you are guaranteeing could sue you in your own name if you refuse to pay.

3. **Insolvent Trading** — the third main way the corporate veil can be pierced is that the entity has been trading insolvent, which means the entity is not able to pay its bills as and when they are due. This does not necessarily mean the entity needs to make a profit, but in the case it makes a loss, the losses

need to be funded so that the entity is keeping up with its bills when they're due. I feel this is quite a significant risk for many small business owners because, unless you're super on top of cashflow from the outset, I believe most business owners fall in and out of insolvency at certain times throughout their business life. The most common times would be getting the business off the ground at the start, where the business is growing fast and needs cash to grow or when there have been significant external forces that effect that industry's trading.

So overall, having a company or a trust or a combination of the two does not necessarily give you full asset protection. Moving along the risk spectrum, you'll see at the far right the idea is that the directors of any trading entities are worth nothing on paper.

What that means is that there are no significant assets in the director's own name, which could mean a few things — that all the assets are held in a spouse's name or held in trusts within the family's control (or a combination of the two).

This means that if the director of the trading entity was to be sued or pursued for bankruptcy, there would actually be no point in doing so — going through the expense of this process, which could easily get into tens of thousands of dollars to pursue, and then to get to the end of the road and then the person actually has no assets to settle a successful claim.

Now, I don't say this to encourage people to be reckless, or gung-ho, but I share these asset protection principles so that in the case where you have the right intentions, but something (or a series of things) goes wrong on the journey, you're ideally not set back to square one as a result of a hiccup here or there.

## Risk Taker vs Asset Holder

**RISK TAKER**

**ASSET HOLDER**

In the previous section I mentioned that the directors of the trading entity have nothing in their own name, but there is a spouse that can have assets or control of other trusts which have assets in the family group. Here is where I'd like to share about the risk taker role and the asset holder role.

It is relevant where you have a spouse, and you're keen to build your family wealth together in a way that preserves your assets in the event of a legal attack. The idea is that the risk taker is the director of the trading entities, therefore dealing with much more risk.

Comparatively, the asset holder does not act as director of any trading entities, but they can be a director of any investment related entities like an asset trust's trustee company, the shareholder of a company (usually via control of a trust), or the ultimate controller of an asset trust, which is called an appointor or principle depending on the deed.

I will also pre-empt a couple of normal questions that pop up when I share this scenario:

### 1. What if I don't have a spouse?

If you don't have a spouse or a partner that you are ready to build assets with together, then, unfortunately, this strategy can be quite limited. You will need to act as both the risk taker and the asset holder in terms of the ordinary roles each would take since there is no one else to take them.

We have had clients use family members in the past, whether it be a parent or a sibling — but I feel this strategy has downsides because there isn't limited protection if your relationship with them sours, and there can also be difficulty with estate planning (more on both of those shortly).

There are options such as the Leading Member options discussed shortly in the advanced asset protection strategies that may be suitable for people with no option for an asset person.

### 2. What happens in the case of divorce?

This question always comes up when I share the idea of having all the assets in 1 person's name and none in the other person's name. In the case of divorce, we check with two family lawyers. Both share the same answer: the assets of both spouses and any trusts they control would likely be considered marital assets if they built them while they were together.

This means that on paper you would have 100% of the assets in 1 person's name or control, 0% in the other person's name — but in the eyes of the family court, they would see them as that marriage's assets. So, I feel there is some form of protection here — but the other thing to remember is that if 1 person owns the family home in their own name, they could essentially sell the family home without sign-off from the other person.

### 3. What do I need to consider with estate planning?

When it comes to estate planning, there are a few things to think when you have this risk taker and asset holder strategy set up. If the asset holder were to pass away, you wouldn't want all the assets transferred into the risk taker's name. This can be avoided with estate planning by using testamentary trusts, meaning the assets of the asset holder end up in a testamentary trust controlled by the risk taker — rather than in the risk taker's name directly. We have a whole lot more information on estate planning in the book Wealth for Life, including more about the benefits of testamentary trusts as well.

### 4. Who should own the family home?

This is a very common question we get from clients. In general, I would recommend if you have an asset holder, then it goes in their personal name only — excluding the risk taker. Note that this means that the asset person is the only one that needs to sign a contract to sell the house. Owning your own home in a personal name will give you access to primary residence exemptions for capital gains tax purposes, along with reduced interest rates from the bank for it being your own home compared to if it was an investment property.

There are instances where some people use the ownership structure of tenants in common, where the risk taker owns 1% of the property and the asset holder owns in 99%. I feel this is still low-risk, although the risk taker will show up if there is a property search done in that person's name. This option means both spouses will need to sign a contract to sell the house.

The other one we see occasionally is the family home being purchased in a trust. The reason someone would do this is if they were further along the risk spectrum, and they wanted next to no assets in anyone's personal name. This comes with downsides, where the trust would not get the main residence capital gains tax exemption when the house was to be sold. You would pay investment interest rates with the bank. The plus side is that you would be able to charge yourself a market rate rent, and can claim all the normal rental property deductions related to the owning and running of your house. The trust would be the investor, and yourselves, as individuals, would be the tenant.

## Advanced asset protection strategies

### 1. Leading member discretionary trust

A leading member discretionary trust is a type of trust with a special deed that gives control to a single person called a leading member (or, in some cases, jointly with another person) for the purposes of having a line of control within a family group.

The idea of a leading member is almost like the line of succession in the royal family. There is a set order of who takes the throne when the current person on the throne dies or becomes incapacitated. While the current person is on the throne, they have ultimate control of what happens.

There are protections in place if that leading member is sued, goes bankrupt, or comes under legal attack, where the successor leading member can replace that initial leading member. This is a great solution if you do not have your spouse as an asset person — it has built-in defences that can pass control onto a trusted family member until the threat has passed.

### 2. Leading member SMSF

A leading member self-managed super fund is a super fund with a special deed (like the trust above) where there is a single person called the leading member that has overall control over the self-managed super fund.

Again, this is a great mechanism to have 1 person of the family group having most of the sway — and a good opportunity to retain control if you would like to have your kids or extended family as part of your self-managed super fund, but you are concerned about the decision-making or leadership of that self-managed super fund.

### 3. The Business Protector (IP entity & licence fee)

Another advanced asset protection strategy is for business assets such as intellectual property or equipment to be owned in a separate entity to the trading entity (the trading entity being the one that interacts with third-party clients and suppliers). This IP or equipment entity then leases its assets to the trading entity.

In the event the trading entity is legally attacked or forced into liquidation, the assets of the IP entity or equipment entity stay intact. It is great for businesses that have a high volume of equipment needed to run their business or serious amounts of money spent on developing software or other intellectual property that would be wise to protect. There are legal mechanisms that need to be in place for this to work, so you need to work with advisers to make sure you tick the right boxes.

### 4. Gift and Loan Back

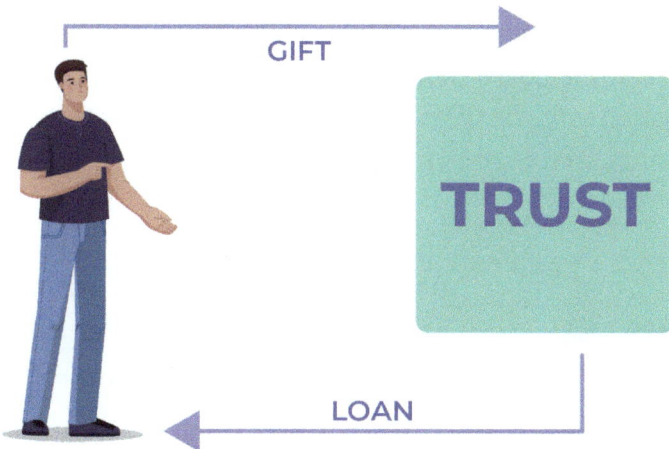

This strategy deals with assets in your personal name. Where possible, and as long as it doesn't cost excessive amounts of tax or stamp duty, I prefer significant assets transferred by their legal title from your personal name into a trust or the asset holder's name. Where this is impractical or expensive, an alternative is the gift and loan back solution. This is where you, as a person, gift an amount of money or equity to a trust, and then you loan that money back from the trust.

Let's say you had $100,000 in cash in your own name. You gift this cash to your trust through a deed of gift. Then if you needed to spend some or all of that money personally, you could draw up a loan agreement — and even better it being a secured loan agreement that the trust is actually lending you the money.

A similar scenario can work with equity that you have in properties including your family home. The rules around this including the legitimacy of these gift and loan back strategies has been reviewed in recent years and will likely come under scrutiny. So please make sure you are working with a good adviser and a lawyer who knows their way around this and review regularly to make sure these agreements are up to date.

### 5. Successor Directors

There is a requirement to make sure that our company has an Australian resident director at all times. When we do structuring, we will often have many companies that only have a single director. The question to ask is, "What happens if that director dies or loses capacity to act?"

There are practical implications for not having a director, including the ability to access bank accounts or legally deal with customers or suppliers. But the other thing to keep in mind is you are breaching the Corporations Act by not having a director for that company. There is a mechanism we can put in place called a "successor director" — which is when you work out in advance who your replacement director would be if you die or are unable to act as the director. This means that you should never have a company that does not have a director — because of this documented outcome should any of the triggers take place.

### 6. Moat and Castle

The Moat and Castle is what we refer to when a client has gone through the process of putting all these pieces together for asset protection. It's the whole box and dice.

The client will likely have the following things in place after we have built the Moat and Castle:

- leading member discretionary trusts and self-managed super funds

- a gift and loan back strategy on personally held assets including the family home

- successor directors in place

- separate business assets into a separate IP or equipment entity with the licensing agreement back to the trading entity

- completed wills with inbuilt testamentary trusts

- power of attorney documents

# Example best practice structures

## 1. Trading Company

**Trading Company**

One of the most common structures setups is a trading company that has a discretionary trust as its shareholder. The company is on the side of risk because it runs the business; the only purpose of the discretionary trust is to own the shares and receive dividends from the company. The benefit of this structure is long-term: you're able to have additional owners buy in or invest in the company without having to completely change the structure.

The sale of shares in the company is also exempt for stamp duty purposes in most circumstances, so another benefit of change is down the track. The downside is that your profits will be taxed in the company first, then paid as dividends to the shareholder in subsequent years.

## 2. Trading Trust

**Trading Trust**

Having a trading trust is another very common structure. We highly recommend for the trading trust to have a corporate trustee if it's running a business. The benefits of a trading trust is that the profits that it earns are taxed in each of the beneficiary's hands, not paid initially by the trust. The benefit of a trading trust is that it does not technically retain profits because it allocates them to beneficiaries — which means fewer net assets in the trading entity

### 3. Asset Trust

**Asset Trust**

Another type of trust you will likely need is an asset trust. An asset trust is there to purely invest or hold assets. So in the trading company example, the owner of the shares in that company is what we call an asset trust. But if you have an investment property or portfolio of shares and we don't want to put that in your own name, then we would often recommend an asset trust.

We are not as passionate about corporate trustees when it comes to asset trusts compared to trading trusts because there are fewer risks in asset trusts — although we still have a preference for it to be a corporate trustee.

### 4. Bucket company

**Bucket Company**

The other part of your structure that you may need along your journey could be a bucket company. We sometimes call bucket companies corporate beneficiaries. They exist to receive distributions from trusts, and retain that distribution. We often see them being used as a second super fund for the family group because they can build up significant assets in a flat taxed environment (of 25% or 30% depending), instead of being paid out to the family members at potentially higher tax rates of 34.5%, 39%, or 47%.

The trust distributions that are paid to a bucket company need to happen in cash or assets otherwise there will be Division 7A requirements on the unpaid trust distribution.

### 5. SMSF

Another great structure is in SMSF for the reasons mentioned in Chapter 4. An SMSF is a great tool, especially for business owners — primarily for the ability to hold your own commercial property that your business rents. Or you can use your SMSF to invest in a business between business partners if you get the right advice in the structuring of it and don't break the rules.

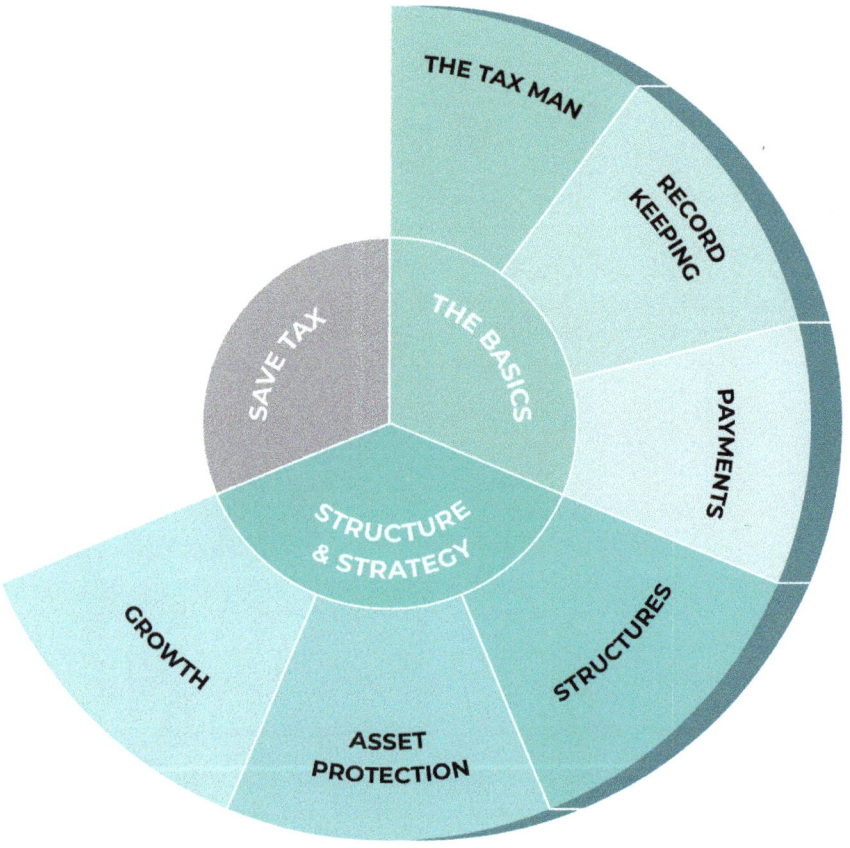

# Chapter 6:
## Growth and Our Structures (And other structure related FAQ)

*"Changing your business structure as it grows is like upgrading from a bicycle to a sports car – suddenly, you've got a lot more horsepower to deal with!"*

**John Smith**

In this chapter, we're going to cover the types of structures you will need or use as your business and life journey grow and go through the different stages.

## The "Rolls Royce" of Structures

We occasionally have clients who come to us in pretty early stages of business that have heard of advanced asset protection strategies or other advanced structuring, and they want us to set them up. However, after we go through our normal structuring advice process, we work out that they probably don't need that level at the stage they're currently at, but we do have a conversation of the likely triggers that will pop them into the next stage of their structuring requirements.

So we don't really want to start a client with the Rolls Royce of structures but rather meet their current and short-term needs. It is also important that when we set up these initial structures, we are being mindful of what they may need over the long term. This is because the way we set up structures right from the start could impact the cost to change the structures as they grow.

## Changing your structure as you go

The first thing that needs to be kept in mind is that your business structures and investment structures can change as you grow. There are some initial structures, like your business trading entity, that you will need as a business owner. But even having an asset trust as your investment structure doesn't need to be set up from the start (unless, of course, you have a need — such as investments — that require a place to sit).

So, when we do our structure and strategy session with our clients, we often go through their immediate needs and then outline some additional structures they might need in the medium- to long-term.

## Typical stages of structures (start-up v growing, v maturing v selling v retiring)

In this next section, we will run through some common stages that your business might go through and what we commonly see for structuring options in each. Please remember, though, that this isn't a prescription for everybody — your needs will be different from the next client group. We always suggest getting personalised advice when it comes to making decisions around structuring from accountants who are specialists in the area you require.

## 1. Start up

The first phase business owners go through is the start-up phase. Often in this phase, business owners want to keep their expenses down — including the initial advice around structuring and the structures themselves. Ideally, if you're going to get a fast growth business or a business that's going to hit a few $100,000 in turnover in the first couple of years, I would recommend investing in a proper business structure from the start.

Example structures that you might want to use here is a company that's owned by a discretionary trust or a discretionary trading trust with a corporate trustee (the discretionary trust recommendation is, of course, assuming there is only 1 family group involved). If you are just testing the idea or you're not sure how it will go and you expect the revenue to be under $100,000 a year, while I still don't love the idea of being a sole trader, it may be best just to do that to keep things simple — until you work out how to produce consistent revenue and make profit out of what you're doing.

## 2. Growing & Maturing

During the next stage, we usually see a business go through a growth stage, or a maturing stage, and they need some additional structuring.

## Allowing for additional investors

One potential option that a client might want is to allow an investor or even an employee to buy into some of their business. If you have a company structure as your trading entity, it is a pretty straightforward process to allow this.

If you start off with a discretionary trust and want to add an investor, you will need to change your trading entity into a new structure. This would mean selling your business from your discretionary trust structure to a newly formed structure: either a company or unit trust can have additional investors owning a fixed interest in your business.

Please note that selling your business from your discretionary trust to another structure will attract capital gains tax and potentially stamp duty consequences. I go into a bit more detail on that shortly in the Changing Your Structure section of this chapter.

## Bucket company

Another entity that you may include in your group of structures is a bucket company. Sometimes we call bucket companies corporate beneficiaries as well. Their purpose is to receive distributions from trusts after money has been allocated to the individuals in the family group, where the balance is allocated to the company to pay tax at a flat rate of either 25% or 30%. This is a great tax management strategy, but also great for asset protection — and the bucket company can use the money it receives for investment purposes.

Just a note — when you invest in a bucket company, you do not receive a capital gains tax discount if you own your investment for more than 12 months. You do get a 50% discount on your capital gains if you own the asset in a trust or in your own name, so you need to weigh up the pros and cons before you make such an investment. This is considered in a similar way to a second super fund, but with fewer rules, and you can access the cash in the bucket company should you need.

To get money out of a bucket company, your choices are either a loan or dividends to the shareholders (this is assuming that your bucket company does not trade and cannot pay a salary). If you loan money from your bucket company, do keep in mind these rules are governed by Division 7A — which make minimum repayments and interest paid.

## Asset Trusts

Another common entity which I've mentioned already in the book is an asset trust. A standard asset trust is a discretionary trust that does not trade. The purpose is to hold assets in the family group. This could be the shares in other companies, the units in other unit trusts, property investments, shares — basically any investment you can think of could end up in an asset trust.

The thing to be mindful of is having all your eggs in one basket: you may want additional asset trusts for different types of investments you make. For instance, you may want an asset trust that holds related party shares and other very low-risk investments in 1 trust, while you own property that has debt attached to it in a separate asset trust.

Some clients even have separate asset trusts for each property or up to a limit of property in each trust. For instance, they max out at $1,000,000 in property value per trust before they set up an additional trust. There are no set rules for all of this — it comes down to your preferences, tolerance to risk, and long-term view.

### 3. Selling

When you're looking to sell your business, there are 2 ways to sell your business in terms of how the sale is structured. You can sell the shares or the units in your company or unit trust to the buyer, and they take on control of that entity. In this case, the shareholder or unit holder of the entity will make the capital gain. If this is the way you sell your business, you will no longer own your trading entity.

The alternative is that they buy the goodwill from your company or trust, and your company or trust makes the capital gain and you retain the entity. If this is the way you sell your business, your trading entity that ran the business will probably be in your control, but now it is not trading after the sale of the business, and the capital gain needs to be dealt with.

There are some great capital gains tax concessions for small business owners. Normally, the tax isn't too scary and there are exemptions, rollovers, and concessions that often can be applied to bring the tax down, even right down to $0 in many cases. There is a whole section in Chapter 9 all about small business capital gains tax concessions.

There aren't too many structure considerations during the sale process itself, although there is a point in the Retiring section shortly on drawing dividends back out from bucket companies because your income will no longer be there from the business.

### 4. Retiring

There are a couple of things to consider with the retirement phase of life and your structures — the main one being any tax implications from winding up entities that you have.

To wind up the entity, usually you need to empty any retained profits out of that structure and allocate them to other individuals or entities in the family group. This process may trigger tax, so it needs to be done with advice.

### *Drawing back out dividends from bucket companies*

You may have a bucket company that has retained earnings from many years of receiving distributions. As I mentioned in the Growth section of structuring, you can get this money back out through either loans or dividends. Loans have Division 7A consequences.

With dividends after retirement, they are usually a great strategy for getting the cash out of bucket companies. This is because often the individuals in the family group are earning much less income in their own names, and when we pay dividends from the company to the individual names, often via a trust as the shareholder, the individual is then taxed on that dividend.

If the dividend is fully franked (meaning that it has prepaid tax attached to it), it is often the case that the individuals will get small refunds of the franking credits attached to those dividends each year. This is a way that you could fund a quasi-pension from your own bucket company — drawing on the cash or investments in the bucket company, while having the tax bill picked up by the franking credits attached.

We've also had situations where the refunds are quite considerable, for instance, the husband and wife receiving between $20,000 and $25,000 per year in refunds of franking credits drawing down on these retained earnings in the bucket company.

## Superannuation Retirement Strategies

We've talked a number of times about superannuation in the book earlier, and when we talk about retirement with structuring, there's some key points to keep in mind.

The first is remembering that when you retire and have reached age 60, then your superannuation balance can be moved to a pension and taxed at 0% on its earnings. What this means is that your earnings in your super fund will be taxed at 0%. If you're earning franked dividends, your super fund should receive a refund of those franking credits (under the current rules at time of publication).

It's worth noting that the 0% tax rate is capped, which is called the transfer balance cap. The transfer balance cap started at $1.6 million and was indexed to $1.7 million on 1st July 2021. Depending on when you are reading this, the transfer balance cap may have changed again. The current rules say it will increase with the index rate in increments of $100,000, so the next threshold will be $1.8 million. Overall, it makes great sense to earn investment income in your retirement in super because of these low tax rates.

You can continue to put money into super even though you are retired. This is something you might do if you have excess money outside of your super and want to invest the extra money in a large tax environment. The rules have changed over the previous few years to remove a lot of the age limitations on putting money into super. Currently, if you are 74 years old or younger from the 2022-23 financial year, you are suitable for all types of contributions into your super. From age 75 years or older, the only contributions you can make to your super fund are mandated employer contributions and the downsizer contributions.

## Changing your structure

There will be times throughout your business journey where it will make sense to change the structure of your trading. This could be to allow for the option of adding an investor, or splitting out your business' assets into an asset holding entity or moving your business' intellectual property into an entity solely set up to hold IP.

It is common to see changes in business structures to assist with family succession from one generation to the next — where the parents who currently own the business sell all or part of the business to their children.

If you are considering changing your structure, please do this with advice to first discuss what the benefits will be versus the downsides, including an estimate of what the tax bill might be to change.

## Tax on changes to your structure

If you're at a point where you want to change your structures, there are a few tax considerations to keep in mind. The first one is stamp duty. Stamp duty is relevant if you sell a business from an entity to another entity, even if it is within the same family group. Or it could be relevant if your business is in a unit trust and you transfer the units from 1 unit holder to another. Shares in a private company don't attract stamp duty when they're transferred unless the company has land as one of its assets over a certain amount.

Each state has its own rules, so I've summarised some of the key points below for each:

- Queensland — Stamp duty applies to the transfer of businesses including the transfer of units in a unit trust that owns a business. The rate of duty is between 0% and 5.75% of the sale value, at a sliding scale. There is a potential stamp duty exemption under certain circumstances where the business is being transferred from a discretionary trust to a company that is wholly owned by the discretionary trust that the business is being transferred from

- New South Wales — Stamp duty has not been charged on business transfers since 2016.

- Victoria — Stamp duty is not charged on business transfers in Victoria either.

- ACT — There is no stamp duty on transfers of businesses.

- South Australia — There is no stamp duty on transfers of business signed after 18th June 2015.

- Tasmania — Stamp duty was removed on business transfers in 2008.

- Western Australia — Stamp duty is payable on the transfer of business assets including goodwill and intellectual property. Rights are between 1.9% and 5.15%, depending on the sale price.

- Northern Territory — Stamp duty is payable on business transfers at a rate of up to 5.95%, apart from the following assets:

  o trading stock

  o manufacturing materials and working progress manufacturing goods

  o livestock

  o motor vehicles

  o cash

The other tax to consider when changing structures is capital gains tax. This is a federal tax so there are no state-based differences. It is also applicable even if you sell a business from your own entity to another entity that you own.

The good news is that there are many capital gains tax concessions for small business owners. I do cover this in detail in Chapter 9 of the book, but broadly speaking, unless you fall outside of the small business capital gains tax concessions, your tax rate usually does not go above 12.5% on the gross capital gain that you make when you sell a business from an entity.

## The process of setting up or changing your structure

I've changed my business structure twice since I started out in 2013. Each time it has been frustrating from an administration perspective because there a lot of moving parts to cover off on. I thought it was worth including a section in the book on what the practical steps are you need to consider when you set up a new entity or you change your structure and need to set up your new trading entity ready to continue running the business.

### Paperwork of new entities

The first thing is to sign the paperwork to set up your company or trust (or a combination of both). This documentation is usually prepared by your accountant, but it needs signatures from the director's shareholders, trustees, and appointors / principals of the trust. At Inspire, we call these signing ceremonies, and it's usually the first step you take before you can go and do the remaining steps to set up your new entity.

Company setups can usually be done electronically. Unfortunately, with trust setups, because the laws are different in each state, we often recommend to sign these with a wet signature. This may change over the next couple of years, meaning potentially all setups could be done electronically, so watch this space.

## New bank accounts

The next step is to set up the bank account for your new entity. At Inspire, we issue a letter to your bank when we create your structure, just so they get the right name on the bank account. If you have a trust with a corporate trustee, we have seen banks set up the name of the bank account in the name of the trustee instead of the trust, which can be quite confusing.

As an example, in our letters, we spell out the exact full name such as:

*Inspire Accountants Pty Ltd ATF Inspire Accountants Trust.*

ATF means "as trustee for". As you can see in the example, there are 2 entities linked by the ATF. This is how the account should be marked when you see it in your bank statements.

Even though we spell this out, we have often seen banks set it up with just the trustee with no mention of the trust, for example:

*Inspire Accountants Pty Ltd*

You will also need to keep your trust deed and company information handy if you are going to set up other accounts with financial institutions, such as online trading platforms, to trade shares.

## ABN, TFN, GST, PAYGW

The next thing accountants should set up for you in the structure setup is the registrations with the ATO. This can be done by the business owner, although it is recommended to be done by the accountant, given they do the process day in, day out. They will need some personal details from the key people in the structure, along with an idea of the type of business that you intend to run.

TFN stands for Tax File Number, and it is something that all entities that earn income need with the ATO. This number should be kept private and not shared with anyone, apart from financial institutions who ask for it.

ABN stands for Australian Business Number. If your structure runs a business, you need this — it is optional for other entities like investment entities, although often not really relevant in day-to-day operations. This number is a public number, and it is searchable on the Australian business register (ABR).

On the ABR, the public record will show the legal entity, the date the ABN was registered, and other tax registrations like GST (Goods and Services Tax) and income tax concessions if they exist. Your bank will likely ask for your ABN when you establish your bank account. If they ask for your ABN but you run an entity that does not trade a business, you do not need to provide an ABN even though they're asking for one. You could provide the TFN if that is a substitute for their system. The reason they ask for this is because the ATO requires them to send information on interest or other income earned directly from the bank to the ATO each year. The ABN and TFN links the right accounts to the right entity with the ATO.

GST, as mentioned above, stands for Goods and Services Tax, and it is a registration that is optional if your business turns over under $75,000 in sales a year. However, it's mandatory if your business turns over more than $75,000 a year or it is projected that your business will turn over more than $75,000 in the following 12 months. We have seen business owners who have not done this correctly, or think it is only once they turn over $75,000 in a financial year, but that is incorrect.

You need to think about what your forecast 12-month period looks like. In the event that you get caught out on this limit, you may need to remit GST on invoices you previously did not charge GST — and this can hurt a lot. GST is disclosed and paid on your BAS which is either an annual, quarterly, or monthly report that needs to be lodged with the ATO, depending on your turnover and registration.

PAYGW stands for Pay As You Go Withholding, and it is the tax withheld on payments to your employees. It is a requirement to register for PAYGW if you employ people using payroll, even if it is yourself. This tax should be calculated by your payroll software (such as Xero). It is payable either monthly or quarterly depending on how much you withhold each year. The disclosure and payment is made on your BAS if your reporting period for PAYGW matches your reporting period for GST as well, or it could be reported and payable on your IAS (instalment activity statement) if you are required to lodge a monthly PAYGW statement, but not GST monthly.

## Business name

Another registration you can make is to register a business name. You need a business name registration if you would like to trade as a name, or be known as a business name that is different from your legal entity. This is a registration done on the ASIC website, and it will be attached to your ABN. The cost is around $40 for a year or $100 for a 3-year registration. Business names are publicly searchable on the Australian business register, in the same place you search for an ABN.

## Clients paying into new bank account

Another thing you'll need to consider is how do you receive money from your clients? If you are a new business, you would likely need a merchant facility or a way to take credit card payments, such as Stripe. These need to be redirected to your new entity's bank account.

If you are an existing business, you need to explore the steps needed with your merchant provider or the software that takes payments from your customers and make sure it is paying into your new entity's bank account.

## Supplier accounts

One of the next things to consider is your supplier accounts. If you're a fresh business, you may only get cash on delivery accounts with suppliers. If you are an established business and you're changing structure, you'll need to notify your suppliers of your change of ABN and legal entity. Unless you have a good relationship with the supplier, this may mean you will need to register a new account as if you are a new business — and potentially lose good trading terms that you were previously on. I feel this varies with different businesses or suppliers, but it is something to consider: that it's a new agreement because you're a new legal entity.

## Patents, Trademarks, Domains (and other IP)

Another thing to consider is the registration or transfer of intellectual property into your new entity. The most common and cheapest one is your internet domain name, which you can register to your new entity's name. If you are transferring patents or trademarks to the new entity or an IP entity, please consult with a lawyer who deals with IP on the best way to do this.

## Shareholders' Agreement

Another structural consideration is implementing a shareholders' or unitholders' agreement (sometimes called a stakeholders' agreement if there are quite a number of entities in the group). This is ideal if you've got more than 1 family group involved in the business because it sets the ground rules and offers legal protections for all parties.

I personally recommend this is a mandatory step for anyone going into business with someone who is not your spouse. They can cost as little as a few thousand dollars. I once heard a good friend say, "Spend the money with the lawyers at the start, not at the end." The idea is that it could save a lot of financial (and emotional) cost down the track if things are agreed on and established in writing at the beginning of the process.

## Structure FAQs

As accountants, we often get questions from clients around the best structure to put different businesses or assets in. Here are a handful of frequently asked structuring questions:

### What structure do I buy the car in?

This is a very common question, and it is quite an easy one if the car is used for business. If you use the car for business, then we want to make sure we maximise our claim for GST and depreciation. This can really only be done in a trading entity, a business asset, or equipment entity that charges a fee to your trading entity for the use of the equipment.

Make sure you keep a logbook recording your business use versus your personal use. You need this information to calculate how much GST and expenses to claim against the car. You need to keep a log book for 12 continuous weeks, and if your driving doesn't change substantially, you can use this percentage for business use for up to 5 years. If the car is for personal use, then the simplest approach is for the car to be purchased in the asset person's name. There is no real incentive to buy it in the business entity.

## What structure do I buy the family home in?

There are 2 main answers for this — the first and most common is putting it in the asset person's name. That is how my own home is structured. It is better protected in the asset person's name rather than in joint names. We often see people buy the family home in joint names because it sounds logical without this knowledge. If your house is owned in joint names, the property will show up on the risk taker's public property holding report, making them a more attractive target to sue if presented the opportunity.

The second option is in a trust. The downside to this is you will be paying investor rates (which are usually higher on your home loan), and you will get no capital gains tax exemption when you sell the property. The upside is if you charge yourself a market rent from the trust, you are able to treat it like an investment property and claim relevant and allowable deductions in the trust.

## What structure do I buy the investment property in?

The answer to this question is mainly answering by asking, where is the best outcome from a tax perspective? It is usually the most flexible option to buy an investment property in the name of a trust; this allows the capital gain to be spread between family members on the eventual sale of the asset. If there is a business that is run where you are able to distribute income to the trust that owns the property, then you can soak up any negative gearing tax losses.

If the property is negatively geared but there is no way to get business income into a trust, it is usually then best to purchase the property in the name of the highest income earner where there will be the maximum tax effect. Keep in mind this can backfire if you make a considerable gain in the future. Sometimes, depending on the overall income or wealth of the family group, we even suggest buying a property in a company name. This is often to assist with Division 7A obligations.

## What structure do I carry out property development in?

Property development, such as subdivisions or knock down and rebuilds, are businesses in themselves. We highly recommend that these are structured in their own company or trust (or combination of both) depending on the requirements and who is involved in the development.

We have even seen situations where the property being developed has been the family home for many years and the clients have transferred the property into another structure before the property development is actually carried out. Structuring a property development is very dependent on a case-by-case basis to what is the best outcome here, so I recommend taking careful advice before you purchase any land or start any development activity.

## What entity should I use for investing money for my kids?

This one is a tricky one because if you purchase investments in your kid's name, you do need to act as the trustee of the money and you will end up paying tax on it. If you purchase the investments in a trust, you can distribute a small amount, which is currently $416 a year to each child before you start paying 47% tax on the balance. We often suggest investing via a trust and working out at the end of each year where the best places are to distribute that income so that you pay the least amount of tax.

The alternative to this is looking into insurance bonds, where the investment is internally taxed at a rate of 30% and is capital gains tax free if held over 10 years. It is best to talk to a financial adviser experienced in investment bonds if this is what you'd like to do.

## What entity do I buy the boat in?

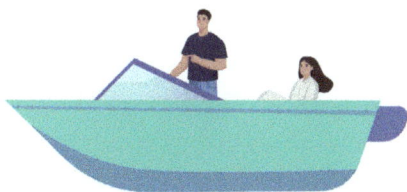

If the boat has nothing to do with your business, then there is no benefit to buying a boat in a business entity. If you have a boat that is used partly (or solely) for business use and partly for personal use, then you may want to explore setting up an entity just to own the boat. This means you may be able to claim a portion of the GST, the purchase costs, and the running and maintenance costs relative to your business use percentage of the boat. I would recommend keeping it simple and buying it in a personal name — but not the risk taker's name.

## How should I invest with family or friends?

With this question, I am assuming that there is more than 1 immediate family group involved. Where this is the case, I would recommend owning investments with non-immediate family or friends in a unit trust or a company, where you can own a fixed percentage of that entity. This is common when we structure property developments. If you are looking to purchase an investment property in a simple way, such as 50/50 ownership, you may look to own this in personal names — but be careful from an asset protection perspective, and don't structure this in the risk taker's name.

# PART 3:
# Save Tax

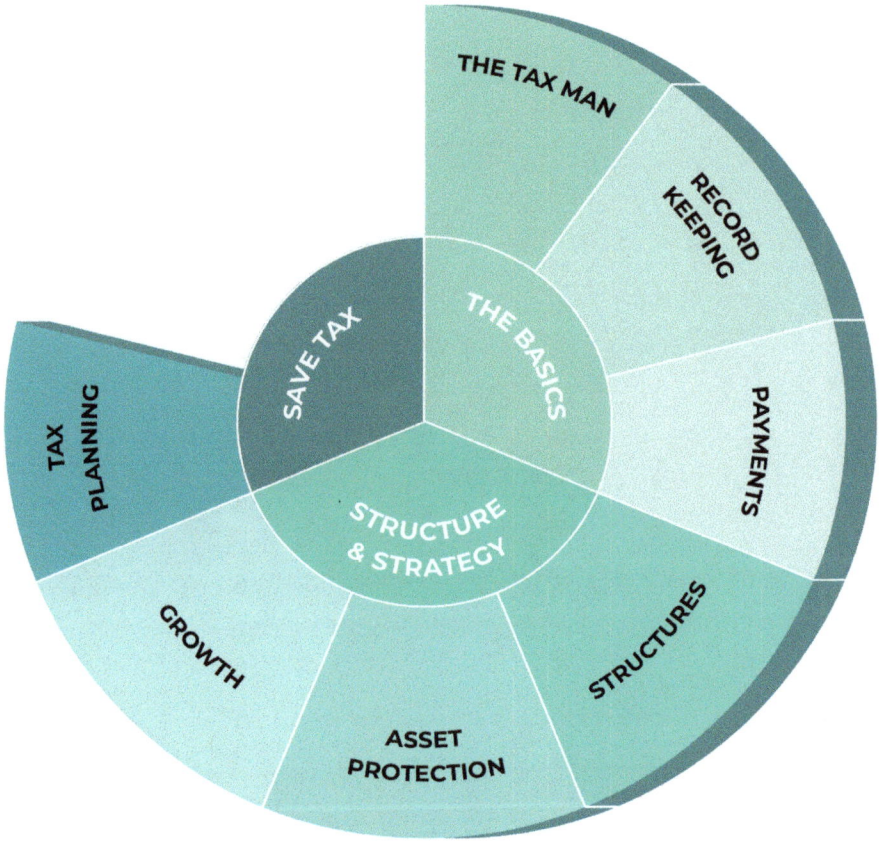

# Chapter 7:
## Tax Planning Process vs Tipping the Tax Man

*"They say a penny saved is a penny earned, but when it comes to taxes, it's more like a dollar saved is a dollar happily pocketed."*

**Sarah Reynolds**

In Part 1 of the book, we discussed the basics of the tax system and the rhythms we need to use. Part 2 covered the structures that we have available in Australia, along with topics around asset protection, and how your structure needs to change overtime. In Part 3, the remaining three chapters are all focused on the way tax works as a business owner, with tips on how to reduce your tax legally.

## The Process of Proactive Tax Planning

I thought it would be good to kick off Part 3 by walking through how we do tax planning at Inspire. Tax planning is an important part of working with our clients throughout the financial year. The tax planning season is from March to June every financial year, and the purpose is to make sure you use every legal strategy you can to pay the least amount of tax possible.

Here are the high-level steps with our tax planning process:

1. To start the process, we put together a list of information we need to help us estimate your business's profit for the full financial year, even though it hasn't finished yet.

   We may also ask questions around your other entities such as the individuals in your family group or other trusts or companies where there is employment or other investment income being earned. We want to make sure we've got a full picture on the estimated incomes of every entity in your family group before we move forward.

2. Soon after step one, we meet with the client to review what we have prepared with the estimates

## What is Tax Planning?

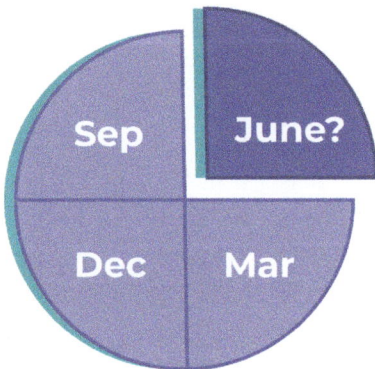

Sep | June?
Dec | Mar

- March to June each year
- Estimate Profit & Tax
- Advise and decide on strategies
- Implement actions

of profit for the year. Through the process, we make some assumptions about what will happen, and these are confirmed or adjusted with the client present.

Once we have our best estimate of profit for each entity and individual in the family group, that gives us the ability to calculate the estimated tax for every entity. We call this the base scenario.

During this meeting, we also discuss the tax planning strategies that are available for the client to reduce their tax bill. The strategies might require cashflow or cash to be paid, and we agree with the client what they are keen to commit to.

We have been able to see the updated estimate of tax payable once these strategies have been applied. We are able to compare this new estimate of tax with the base scenario and show the client the tax savings between the 2.

3. The final step after meeting with the client is to compile a list of action points for both ourselves and the client to complete.

   Usually this is time-sensitive and needs to be completed before 30th June in the relevant financial year. It is extremely important that this action list gets done — both on our side, but particularly by the clients. If there is money to move, it is crucial to get it done before the cut-off date of 30th June.

   Along with the list of action points, we also send through some key documents depending on the family group (you'll find more detail on each of these in further in this chapter):

- Group Tax Summary — this is the summary of the client's family group (inclusive of all entities and individuals) on a single Excel spreadsheet. It shows a summary of the income, along with the estimated tax.

- Trust distribution minutes — this is the document that is required to record who in the family group receives the income from trust. It must be decided on every year if there is income in that trust, recorded and, ideally, signed before 30th June.

- Dividend minutes — part of tax planning may include discussions around paying dividends from companies. If that is agreed on, there are minutes to prepare in order to document this.

## Inspire's Group Tax Summary

The group tax summary is what we use at Inspire to put all of the entities and individuals in the family group on a single spreadsheet. It shows a high-level breakdown over the income and expenses; then this provides the taxable income for each entity before any distributions or dividends.

The next section is the distributions and dividends, where we can allocate profit between different entities in the family group and have immediate feedback of what the total profit after the distribution would be for each entity.

There are formulas inside it to calculate an estimated tax payable as well, so this is a very handy sheet to do tax planning with. It's also useful because it gives a summary of the incomes in a family group — especially where the distributions have gone. This usually sits at the front of our document signing pack when we do year-end financials and tax returns, and it forms the main part of our conversation when we are delivering year-end tax. It is also very handy when discussing with mortgage brokers how you earn income in a business structure.

## Trust distribution minutes

Trust distribution minutes is the document that is required to record who receives the profit of the trust. It is a document that has to be completed by 30th June in the financial year, every single financial year that the trust earns income.

Technically, the rule is that if the trustee does not decide where the profit gets allocated, then the trust, in a way, retains that profit and will effectively pay tax at 45%. The minutes are relatively simple in the idea, although are usually 1 or 2 pages long.

We need to check how income is described in the trust deed because this has an impact on exactly how much of the taxable income we allocate to each person. What I mean here is that there are different types of income: the two main ones are accounting income and taxable income.

Accounting income is income per the financial statements, while taxable income is the income once you take that accounting income and do any tax adjustments to that, such as adding back non-deductible expenses, or taking away other tax-deductible expenses. Sometimes these are the same amount, but often when there is a business that is run, there are adjustments that need to be made here.

Regarding the trust distribution minutes, we need to be careful because with tax planning, we want to consider taxable income only distributed to other people or entities, so we need to be careful that when the trust deed specifies income, if it is not explicitly taxable income, then we must refer to that in the trust distribution minutes. This can get very technical, but I wanted to highlight that it's not just a simple form to fill out — there are additional steps we need to take to get this right.

## Allocating profits in the family group: 10 distribution targets for trusts

We've talked about trust distributions, but what I'd like to run through here is where we normally make those trust distributions.

### Read the deed!

When I run workshops, there are usually ten different beneficiary types I talk about. There are 6 types of people in 4 different types of entities, and I've made some notes on each below.

Each of these beneficiaries does not necessarily need to be named by their legal entity name inside the trust deed, but if they are not named specifically, the category of person or entity needs to be named to allow distribution.

For instance, you may set up a trust before you have children. Your children's names might not be on the original trust deed as beneficiaries, but they may be included under secondary beneficiaries because secondary beneficiaries include children of the primary beneficiaries (that is assuming you are listed as a primary beneficiary).

Sometimes we see companies included by way of referring to "any company that the primary beneficiaries are a director or a shareholder of are included as beneficiaries of the trust".

## The 10 Targets

So here are the ten example beneficiaries that you might consider distributing to:

1. **You** — this is an obvious one where your trust distributes see you as the business owner. The magic number we usually aim for maxing out at is $120,000 because this is where the tax rate goes from 34.5% up to 39% on every dollar between $120,000 and $180,000.

2. **Your spouse** — your spouse may be the next most obvious person to receive distributions from the business. Just keep in mind any other income your spouse earns if they don't work in the business but there are employed.

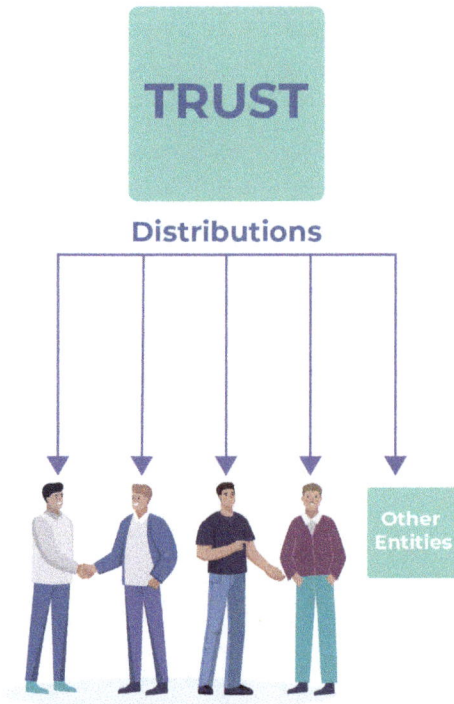

3. **Children** — children under 18 can receive a small amount of $416 and pay no tax on it. Every dollar over that amount, they will pay a 47% tax rate if it is money received from a trust. If they have a job, this income is not taxed at the high rates, but it particularly addresses investment income given to children. If your children are over 18, they are taxed as adults, where around the first $22,000 you give them is taxed at 0%, assuming they have no other income. For children over 18, keep in mind any employment income they might have or HECS/HELP debts if they are studying and accumulating a HECS/HELP debt.

4. **Self-funded retired parents** — self-funded parents are usually able to receive distributions from trusts,

but it is always good to check with the trustee if this is possible. If your parents are receiving an old age pension, they will usually lose this if you distribute a considerable amount from your trust. If it is only a small amount that you distribute to them while they receive a pension, they may be required to report a lot of administrative information to Centrelink about your trust, which, in itself, could be annoying to the point you just don't bother distributing to them. The other thing to watch with parents is any other investment income they have in their own name, like shares or investment properties, which may affect their taxable income before your distributions.

5. **Self-funded retired grandparents** — we can use the same thought process and notes for self-funded retired parents as we can for self-funded retired grandparents. The point with grandparents is they may not be as commonly included as potential beneficiaries in the trust deed as your own parents, so make sure they are included as beneficiaries, otherwise you may want to amend your trust deed to include them.

6. **In laws** — the in-laws could be your parents, or sister, or brother-in-law. If they are your parents-in-law, again, it is good to make sure it is allowable under the deed — but also keep in mind it may not be worth it if they're receiving an old age pension or

any other income they might be receiving. If we're thinking of our brother or sister-in-law, please keep in mind any family tax benefits might be reduced or taken away if you distribute a considerable amount from your trust to them. We've seen childcare rebates or family tax benefits reduced or removed unknowingly on occasions when business owners have distributed to brothers or sisters or their in-laws that have young kids.

7. Superannuation — we don't necessarily distribute from a trust to superannuation directly, but rather the profit from the trust may be distributed to a person, and then they make a personal super contribution that is tax deductible. I've already spoken about this at length earlier in the book, but just remember that the current concessional contribution limit per person is $27,500 each financial year.

8. Church or Charity — I'm referring to two broad types of not-for-profit entities here — the first is a charity, and the second is churches. If you're looking to give money to a charity, any type of business structure (individual, company, trust) can make a donation to a charity that is registered as a deductible gift recipient and it can be claimed as a tax deduction. There are two things you need for this, which is a tax invoice to show the proof, and also the donation has to be more than $2. Donations cannot be claimed as a tax deduction where the amount of the deduction would incur a tax loss.

For churches that are exempt from income tax through an income tax concession, a trust can distribute to the church from pre-tax money. You cannot distribute from pre-tax money as an individual or a company.

You can donate by way of cheque if a charity is a deductible gift recipient or if a church is exempt for income tax purposes by checking the church or charity's ABN on the Australian business register (https://abr.business.gov.au/)

9. **Loss making entity** — about a year into running Inspire, I set up a cafe in the foyer of our new office. I called it Inspire Café. From a structuring perspective, it was set up in a separate trust to the accounting firm. Unfortunately, the cafe made a huge loss in the first couple of years it ran, to the point where I ended up shutting it down. But the good thing is, I was able to offset those losses by distributing profit from the accounting firm's trust into the cafe's trust that made the losses. If you have a trust that makes profit and another company or a trust that makes a loss or has previous losses, you may be able to distribute to that loss making entity to get some tax benefit back from those losses. Be sure to get advice around this as there are additional rules it may prevent it.

10. **Bucket company** — this is lucky last for a reason. A bucket company or a corporate beneficiary is something that we consider giving trust distributions to when we have worked through the potential to

distribute to all the other entities and individuals in a family group. The reason why we would consider giving the trust distributions to our bucket company is because the bucket company pays a flat rate of tax at either 25% or 30%, depending on the structure set up. This is unlike the individual tax rates where the more you earn, the higher your tax rate will be. This is a way for a family to cap their tax at a certain rate. Do keep in mind the cash actually needs to go to the bucket company's bank account eventually, otherwise there may be unintended Division 7A consequences.

## New Guidance from ATO on Trust Distributions - S100A

I wanted to include a bit of a warning because in 2022, the ATO issued controversial guidance around legislation that was brought in decades ago.

Their perspective has seemed to change even though the legislation has not, and the result is a feeling of attacks on commonly used trust strategies. They have also clarified their guidance around what we would consider as borderline tax avoidance before their guidance came out — but also grouping in relatively normal transactions as well.

The gist of what they are trying to crack down on are situations where the people or entities that the taxable trust distributions are made to do not match who ends up with the economic benefit of the trust distributions (or, in other words, who ends up with the cash).

At Inspire, we have been recommending that our clients transfer the cash that their trusts allocate through a distribution to their beneficiaries for years now – and it appears loud and clear that this is the ATO's stance. Therefore, when you are considering your trust distributions, please, firstly, make sure you are working with an accountant who understands their way around this new approach the ATO are taking, but also keep in mind that the way you may have done things in the past needs to adjust if it does not align.

## Dividend minutes

Another document that we may produce if you have a company in your family structures are dividend minutes. These are to document dividends that you may choose to pay from your company's retained profits throughout the year. We do this to get money out of companies to the shareholders. If the shareholder of the company is a trust, these dividends are usually paid to the owners of the business personally, to take money out of the business structures.

They can also be used to pay from a trading entity down to a bucket company or a holding company to retain the profits in a non-trading company. The benefit of this is that you could move these to another structure that is safe from business risk without any or much top up tax to get them there. If your trading company pays tax at

25%, your bucket company may pay tax at 30%; therefore, you might have 5% top tax. Although if you use a trading company 100% owned by a holding company, it is likely that the holding company can adopt to the 25% tax rate as well.

## Tax planning is not once a year

While we start the process for our tax planning in March and finish up by 30th June each year, I do want to suggest a mindset shift when it comes to tax planning. This is especially relevant for new business owners — but we need to keep in mind tax throughout the year, not just in the weeks before 30th June.

The reason for this is if we've just started the business, but we haven't set up a structure yet, I'd hate you to find out in May or June in that financial year that you should have started a company or a trust a lot sooner — and, as a result, you're going to pay 39% or 47% tax on a majority of your profit.

Another potential way you might get into strife is if throughout the year you're making financial decisions without considering the best way to do it from a tax perspective. Whether it's buying a car, an investment property, investing into a portfolio of shares — the timing and the way we do these things can make a big difference from a tax perspective.

At Inspire, we want our clients to reach out before they make important decisions to get our input. It is a big reason why we include quick phone calls or emails at no cost — as most of the above is just a quick confirmation or quick guidance to a client and can mean $1,000s in savings if done correctly versus incorrectly.

In the next chapter, we will dive deep into some of the tax savings strategies that we use at tax planning time, but also things we consider throughout the year when working with our clients and advising them on the ground.

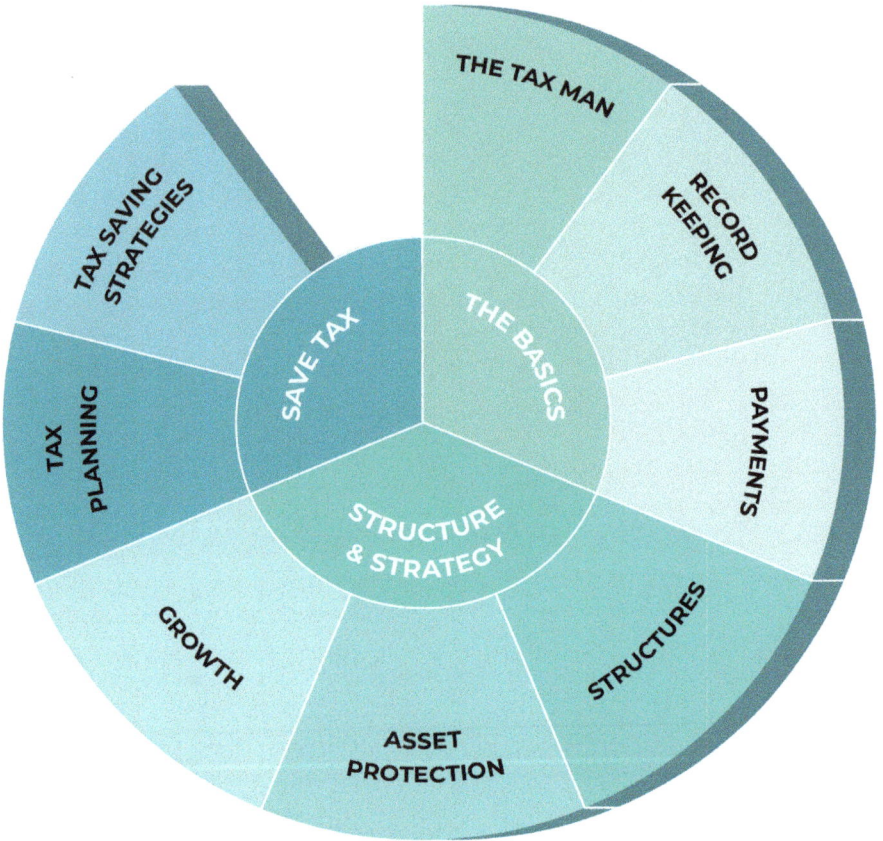

# Chapter 8:
## Tax Saving Strategies

*""In the world of taxation, saving tax isn't just a strategy; it's a financial game plan for keeping more of what you've earned."*

**Anonymous**

## General tax planning strategies

In this chapter I'm going to get stuck into some common tax saving strategies that we use in tax planning time. These are in addition to the structuring that we do when someone starts a business or when a client starts working with us, and we give them some feedback on their existing structures. This list is definitely not an exhaustive list, but it does contain the most common strategies that we use.

The other thing to note is that these strategies are the ones where we find errors when we check a prospective client's most recent set of tax returns that their current account has prepared. We call that process a look under the hood (a second opinion on their tax).

The result of that process is 1 of 2 things:

1) We find that the client has in fact paid tax already — tax that they otherwise wouldn't have needed to pay had they been already working with us.

2) We give them the feedback that they were paying the right amount of tax, and not a cent more.

Unfortunately, for most clients, the majority of the look under the hoods that we conduct result in that first outcome — where we find overpaid tax. The tax savings can easily get close to anything from $10,000 to $20,000, and I do remember a few instances that were up near $100,000 in tax savings.

I know that's a lot of money for most business owners — and I do want to say that the following strategies aren't terribly complex, but they are often missed or done without maximising the tax benefit.

## *Paying tax on money you haven't received yet*

This strategy is relevant for smaller service-based businesses. The idea here is that you are better off paying tax on your sales in the financial year that you actually receive the money, rather than the year that you send the invoice. We call it the receipts-based method of declaring income.

There is no black and white on where you can use the rules for this one as the guidance is using a tax ruling

(TR 98/1). As a guide, it is relevant for small service-based businesses. And in terms of turnover, I would look to see if you qualify if your turnover was less than $1,000,000 (although that is not a legislated limit). The benefit of it is, say, you were owed $100,000 plus GST from clients by 30th June in a financial year; using the receipts-based method would mean you don't need to pay the tax on it until the following financial year assuming you received that money in the next financial year.

In this example with a 30% tax rate, this would mean a $30,000 tax deferral to the following financial year. And if the circumstances of your business qualified you for the receipts-based method in that next financial year, you could defer the tax on any amount owing the following year as well. You apply the test to your income separately from your expenses — which means that you have the option with your expenses whether to claim them as deductions when they are paid in cash or when they are incurred to your business.

## *Claiming Depreciation Correctly*

The rules for claiming depreciation as a small business owner have changed so many times since I started in accounting in 2007.

Broadly there are two types of depreciation:

1) The depreciation on furniture and fittings and equipment that you use every day in your business. This depends on the effective life of the asset, but these assets are usually written off using a diminishing

value over their effective life. Diminishing value just means that there is a higher depreciation in the first few years and then it flattens out for the later years of the effective life of that asset.

2) Then there is depreciation on the cost of construction of buildings, office fit outs, etc. Typically, these expenses are written off for 40 years or 2.5% each year for 40 years.

The current small business rules allow access to simplified depreciation rules for small businesses with a turnover of $10 million or less.

One of the COVID measures introduced was to allow a temporary full expensing of depreciable items (not construction or fit outs). The relevant dates are for any assets purchased between the 6th October 2020 and 30th June 2023. What this meant is that if you had a work ute that was 100% business use, you could claim the full GST exclusive cost of the ute in 1 single financial year, instead of previously using the small business general pool.

From 30th June 2023, the rules reverted back, similar to what they were previously. The way this works is you assign your assets into a general pool and deduct new assets by 15% in the first year, then all other existing assets by 30% every year. The limit is now $20,000 for assets purchased after 30th June 2023 – anything under this amount we can write off immediately, and over $20,000 we need to assign to this general pool. We can likely rely on this amount for the full 2024 financial year!

If you are reading this book after 30 June 2024, please check what the current instant asset write-off limit is.

## *Using a Trust*

When I say using a trust, it's not that you must run your business in a trust structure — but a key sign for being set up well is having a trust in some part of your structure, whether it is your trading entity or maybe you have a company that is owned by a trust. Without a discretionary trust in the family group, it is a sign that the business structure is likely inflexible from a tax planning perspective, and that, in some way, the income from the business structures would likely have a fixed way of ending up in personal names and being used personally.

A mistake we commonly see is a trading company where the shares are held by the person running the business, sometimes the director. This means the person is not only the risk taker while being a director, but they are also the only one who can receive dividends from that company.

If they had a spouse who is not working in the business, even though the spouse may share the economic benefit from that business structure, it would be hard to use the tax thresholds of the spouse to share business income to which would ordinarily reduce the overall tax that family paid. The spouse could not receive a salary if they are not working in the business — and they could not receive dividends as they do not own the shares.

The way a trust would help in this situation is if the trust owned the shares in the trading entity. The trust could then receive dividends from the company and, with this dividend income, it could use its discretion to pay its income to the spouse, using up their tax thresholds. So in my opinion, if you don't have a trust forming some part of your business structures, you are likely setting yourself up for failure from a tax planning perspective at some stage in the future (if not already).

## Ensuring Family Members are in the same Tax Bracket

When we have a good business structure in a family group, there are ways to ensure that all the adult family members are in the same tax bracket. The benefit of this is that you don't have, say, 1 spouse who is pushing into the top tier 47% tax bracket earning $200,000, while the other has $20,000 of income and is paying no tax.

If the couple need to be taxed on $220,000 of income, ideally, and where there are no other special rules that apply, it is best to just give half the income to each spouse. That way each of their incomes are $110,000.

The table below illustrates this with numbers:

|  | SCENARIO 1 | | SCENARIO 2 | |
| --- | --- | --- | --- | --- |
|  | Income $ | Tax $ | Income $ | Tax $ |
| Spouse 1 | $200,000 | $64,667 | $110,000 | $28,417 |
| Spouse 2 | $20,000 | $0 | $110,000 | $28,417 |
| Total | $220,000 | $64,667 | $220,000 | $56,834 |
| Total Tax Savings | | | $7,833 | |

The tax in the table above is a quick estimate using 2024 FY rates.

## *Distributing to a Bucket Company*

A strategy we use to cap a family group's tax rate out at either 25% or 30% is to distribute to what we call a bucket company. For Inspire, a bucket company is a company whose sole purpose is to receive distributions from other entities and invest the money from there. The bucket company can invest by way of earning interest on loans to other entities in or outside of the family group, or it can even invest itself.

If a bucket company invests itself, consideration needs to be given to that investment not receiving the general 50% CGT discount if the investment is held for more than 12 months. This is because companies are not able to use this discount, whereas individuals and trusts are able to use it. (Trusts cannot distribute a 50% general discounted capital gain to a company and it remain discounted; when the company receives a discounted gain, it must gross up the gain again and pay tax on the gross gain.)

In terms of how much to distribute to a bucket company, often we distribute what the family needs, providing cost of living to the individuals in their own names, and with any excess, we can distribute to a bucket company and pay that flat rate of tax. There is no limit on how much we can distribute, apart from the requirement that the cash must follow the distribution or otherwise the entities must comply with Division 7A requirements.

## *Salaries paid to Owners*

There are a handful of things to consider with this one – tax is one of them. You cannot pay an uncommercially high salary to a family member or relative if there is a high level of tax benefit for doing so. Back in the day, we often heard of doctors paying their spouses $100,000 for "bookkeeping". Yeah righto — that's not going to fly with the ATO, so we need to keep this in mind for businesses that are paying salaries to family members working in the business. If they are not working in the business or providing value to it, I would suggest not to pay them a salary: there may be other ways for them to receive taxable income from the business entity, such as dividends or distributions.

But let's say both spouses are working in the business — we want to make sure the salaries are appropriate. Too high, and the personal tax bill will be huge. Too low, and we may get tricked up with Division 7A legislation. Ultimately, there's no hard and fast rules of how much to pay in salaries, so it's important to get advice from your accountant on this and consider all these factors.

## *Prepayments Prior to 30th June*

Small businesses are able to claim a tax deduction for business expenses that have been prepaid for up to 12 months ahead of when it's paid for. As an example, some clients may prepay their rent for 12 months and be able to claim a deduction for it in the year it was paid — even though the period of rent of the expense means it hasn't been incurred to the business yet.

Please note that this strategy only brings forward your tax deduction to the financial year which is about to finish, and it means you'll have a higher tax bill as a result instead in the following year. Unless, of course, you prepay that expense each year. It is a way we can balance out a client's "big" years of profit if that is the case, or we can also manage the cashflow for tax if that is what they'd like to do.

Another thing to keep in mind — say it's coming up to 30th June and you know you'll have some business travel in August or September, booking and paying for the travel in June will mean that the tax deduction you were entitled to would be claimable in the year about to finish versus the next one if you had waited until July to pay.

## Contributions to super

We learned earlier in the book that superannuation is a low-tax environment. So it's not uncommon to find that clients want to get a fair amount of their money inside super so it is growing tax effectively.

There are a number of things to consider when putting money into super.

### Different types of contributions

The 2 main types of contributions are:

- Concessional contributions
- Non-concessional contributions

*Concessional contributions* are contributions that are generally paid "before tax" from your employer or you personally, and a tax deduction is claimed for the contribution. These include your employer contributions, salary sacrifice contributions, and you can make personal concessional contributions too.

When the super fund receives a concessional contribution, it must pay tax on that contribution. Ordinarily the tax rate is 15% (unless there is excess contributions or Division 293 tax).

*Non-concessional contributions* are generally contributions that are made from after tax money, and no tax is paid when the contributions are received by the super fund (unless there is excess contributions). Also, no tax deduction can be claimed for non-concessional contributions.

*Important: Please note that there are age limits and even certain maximum balance limits that apply to contributions, so it is important to understand all the rules and tax impacts before making contributions. I strongly recommend getting advice specific to your circumstances before making any decisions and contributions to super.*

## Contributions caps

There is a limit on the number of contributions that you're able to make into super. This is, in a way, to limit the dollars that are in super being taxed at a lower amount. (I remember there was a year early in my career that you were able to make a $1,000,000 tax deductible contribution into super. That's unreal compared to today's limits.)

The current concessional contribution cap is $27,500 per financial year per person.

The current non-concessional contribution cap is $110,000 per financial year per person.

These amounts are indexed in step-ups in amounts of $2,500 or $10,000, respectively, and there are special rules in certain circumstances for putting additional amounts into super. More on that now.

## Carry Forward unused concessional cap

From the 2019 financial year, a new rule was brought in: if you had unused concessional contributions and you meet certain conditions, you're able to carry that unused amount forward for up to 5 financial years.

The basic rules are that you must have less than $500,000 in super at the start of the year in which you use the carry forward rule and also be under the age of 67 — or if you are between the ages of 67 and 75, you need to have satisfied the work test during the year you make the carry forward contribution. You must use your current year's contribution cap before allocating it to the oldest available year in which you have unused cap.

## Bring Forward non-concessional cap

There is a special rule for non-concessional contributions where you may "bring forward" from future years' caps your non-concessional contributions amount. This applies to the current year, plus the following 2 financial years' caps.

So, if we used today's limit of $110,000, that's $110,000 x 3 years or $330,000.

The year in which you trigger it starts that 3-year period by which you cannot trigger a further bring forward rule. You must be 74 years old or younger at the time in which you make the contribution, and your super balance must be under certain limits. However, generally, you are fine if your balance is under $1,680,000 in the current 2024 financial year.

## Tax planning strategies as a high-income employee

We had a question from a client, not about structuring for his business, but what his wife could do from a tax planning perspective. The husband runs a business and earns a solid $150,000 profit. Through proactive tax planning, we ended up saving him over $35,000 in tax, keeping his average tax rate on the business income less than 25%.

Great! He loved that, so what about his wife? His wife earns $250,000 as an employee. This means she's paying 47% tax on a good portion of that income, but an average tax rate of about 35% on each dollar she earns. Not cool. Unfortunately, there's not as many things you can do to plan for tax as an employee compared to a business.

And I would NEVER recommend spending $1 on something tax deductible to save 47 cents in tax just for the tax savings.

(Although it sounds tempting — remember you lose 53% of what you're spending money on.)

So, what are the top tax planning strategies for high income employees? Here's our list of 9 things to consider:

## 1. Contribute to your Superannuation Fund

The first way you can reduce your taxable income (and therefore your tax on that income) is through additional superannuation contributions. We spoke about this in detail in the previous section, but here's some things to remember in this specific case:

Be careful to not exceed your contribution cap for deductible superannuation contributions.

These deductible super contributions include both your employer minimum (mandatory 11% they have to pay on your salary) plus any salary sacrifice or additional contributions that you do. The current annual concessional cap is $27,500. Going over the caps mean you pay an effective tax rate of whatever your outside of super marginal tax rate is anyway.

Crunching the numbers, let's imagine that your employer already chipped in $22,500 so far in the tax year as (the minimum they need for your salary), and you have $5,000 that you could contribute, taking you up to the cap. You'd have to contribute $5000 of money into super, but it would save you $2,350 outside of super tax by doing so (if you were paying 47% tax on your salary). It's always talk to a good financial advisor to make sure this is appropriate for your situation.

## 2. Negatively Gear an Investment Property

Another very common scenario is that high income earners have a negatively geared investment property. What this means is that the tax deductions they get from renting out the property outweigh the rental income they receive from the property.

This could be $25,000 in rent received, less $20,000 in expenses paid for during the year (like interests on loans, council rates, agent's fees), and then a further deduction of $20,000 for depreciation on the property. Under this scenario, while the property "made" $5,000 net in positive cash flow, the property made a taxable loss of $15,000. If you're paying tax at 47%, this negative gearing would reduce your tax bill by $7,050.

## 3. Get Private Health Insurance

Having private health insurance (hospital cover) means that you do not have to pay the Medicare levy surcharge. There's often confusion when clients have hospital cover, but they still pay Medicare Levy. That's because there are two types of Medicare payments on your tax:

- Medicare levy (it is calculated at 2% of your taxable income if you're earning more than ~$24,000 and you don't have any exemption or reduction)

- Medicare levy surcharge (additional 1% to 1.5% depending on your income)

You need to pay the surcharge component if you're single and earn over $93,000. You also need to pay if you have a spouse and together your income combined is more than $186,000 and you don't have private health insurance (hospital cover). Of course, if you (or you and your spouse) do hold the hospital cover, you do not have to pay the surcharge component.

If you earn $300,000, you'd be up for $4,500 in Medicare levy surcharge alone — and hospital cover may only cost you $2,500 to take out! On that maths, you'd be better off by $2,000.

So if you're over the income threshold ($93,000 if you're single or $186,000 if you have a spouse, incomes combined), or are creeping toward it, it may be worth taking out cover.

And just as an FYI — having only private health insurance (extras cover) does not remove the surcharge.

## 4. Salary sacrifice your vehicle

Some people salary sacrifice a vehicle that they use both for business and private use — this can usually shave a few hundred, or a few thousand off your tax bill. This usually looks like your employer organising a novated lease, operating lease, hire purchase, or paying for your car. There are many ways to structure it depending on what your employer is comfortable with — and we recommend getting advice on what option is best for you and your employer at the time.

There have even been rules brought in recently allowing you to salary sacrifice an electronic vehicle and it is also fringe benefits tax exempt. There are certain requirements of the vehicle, but it is an option which can save thousands on tax.

## *5. Donate to Charity*

If giving is something you do, or want to do, then consider making a tax-deductible donation.

As an employee, you can claim a donation of anything over $2, to an Australian Deductible Gift Recipient (DGR), as long as you get a tax invoice from them. To work out if a charity is a DGR, you can check the Australian Business Register here: http://abr.business.gov.au/

Once you search for your charity and find it, you can look down the bottom of the search and the Deductible Gift Recipient status will show up:

Donating or "tithing" to churches cannot be claimed as a tax deduction on an individual tax return, unless it is a

---

**Deductible gift recipient status**     help

AUSTRALIAN RED CROSS SOCIETY is endorsed as a Deductible Gift Recipient (DGR) from **01 Jul 2000**. It is covered by Item 1 of the table in section 30-15 of the *Income Tax Assessment Act 1997*.

AUSTRALIAN RED CROSS SOCIETY operates the following funds, authorities or institutions. Gifts to these funds, authorities or institutions may be deductible.

| Fund, authority or institution name | DGR Item | From |
|---|---|---|
| AUSTRALIAN RED CROSS BLOOD SERVICE | Item 1 | 01 Jul 2000 |
| AUSTRALIAN RED CROSS SOCIETY_DEVELOPING COUNTRIES AID FUND | Item 1 | 01 Jul 2000 |

special fund of the church that is considered a DGR – and a church's building fund is a common example of this.

## 6. Income protection insurance

If you're ballin' on 6 figures or more of salary, it's probably a good idea to protect your income, especially if you're the sole earner in the family or have loan repayment obligations each month — that if you, all of a sudden, found yourself out of work, you'd have trouble paying. You can do this through taking out income protection insurance.

While we do not offer advice on how much to take out and what cover you need, we know that if the policy is paid personally, we can claim the premiums as a tax deduction. If you need help with this, reach out and we can put you in touch with some great people who can help.

## 7. Self-Education, Training or Executive Coaching

If extra study or developing your skills are of interest to you, then you can pay for self-education, professional development, or training and claim this on your tax. You could also hire an executive coach to help you perform better in your role.

Keep in mind that there has to be direct connection with the training and what you do as an employee. For instance, if you have HR responsibilities at work and want to do a training course on how to manage people better, then this would be deductible. But if you're in a sales role and want to learn how to fly a plane (which has nothing to do with your employment), then sorry, that's not deductible.

## 8. Structure Investment Income Appropriately

We often see highly paid people build wealth over years. It's critical that the ownership of any investments (such as interest earning bank accounts, shares, investment properties) is carefully considered. Whoever owns these assets and receives the income pays the tax on that. So if a wife owned the assets, she'd pay 47% in tax on the investment earnings, compared with, say, the husband at a rate of 39% — a big difference.

Be careful with restructuring investments that you own at the moment, as shifting between family members or entities usually triggers capital gains tax, or stamp duty (or both!). It's best to chat with an accountant who understands this stuff before making any decisions!

## 9. Change the way you get paid

The biggest and best way we've seen highly paid, high-functioning people reduce their tax is through changing the way they get paid. The most common way is to start a business consulting to other similar businesses who need their skill, knowledge, or service and building a business from there.

Note that you cannot simply register an ABN and get a couple of clients to be able to treat your income as if it's come from making profit from a business — consulting income generally needs to end up in the name of the consultant. But if you had a team delivering the consulting while you ran the business (even consulting for part of it yourself), then subject to certain rules, we can look at the tax advantages of trusts and companies.

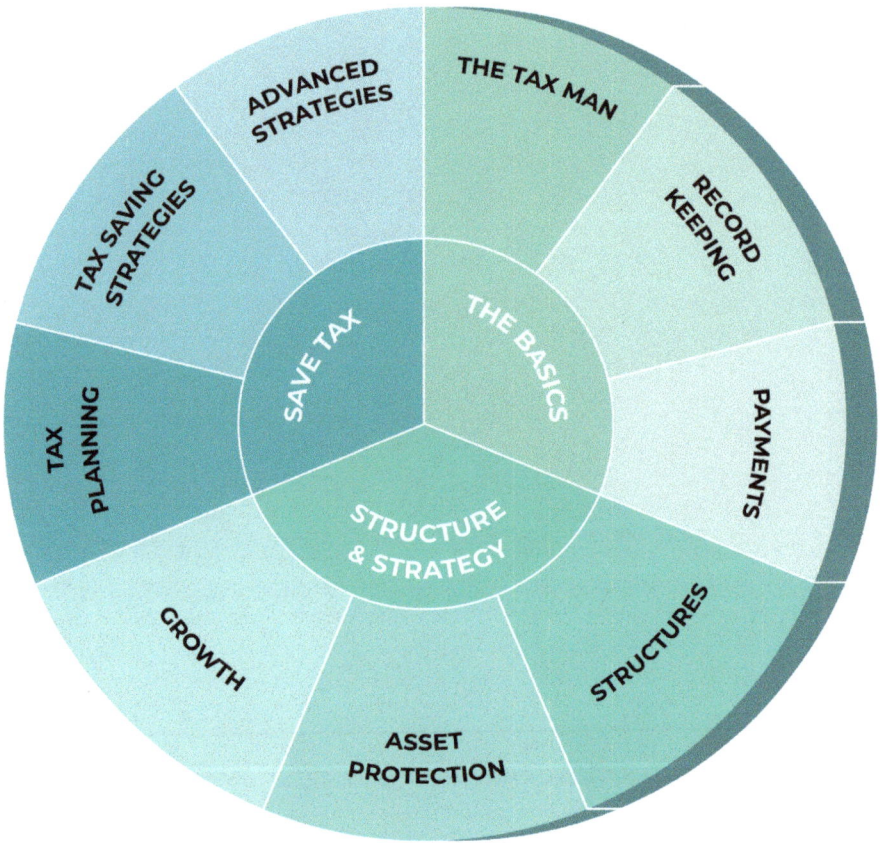

# Chapter 9:
## Advanced Concepts

*"When you dive into advanced tax concepts, you're not just treading water; you're swimming toward a sea of financial possibilities."*

**Olivia Turner**

In this chapter, I'd love to dive into a few different advanced concepts or topics when it comes to working with business owners. Not all of these will apply to everyone, but understanding a little about each thing will allow you to be prepared in not only identifying an issue, but also the ability to know what the best next step might be to deal with it. (There's no better substitute, though, than working with a good accountant who can guide you through this.)

The topics below are in no specific order of importance, so I've popped them into alphabetical order to make it easy to refer back to this chapter if needed.

## Allocation of Professional Firm Profits

Allocation of professional firm profits refers to rules brought in over the past few years to determine how profits from a "professional firm" are allocated within a family group. You must follow the guidelines here to avoid ATO scrutiny or them deeming that you are avoiding or evading tax. Generally, they don't want to see structures set up for the sole or dominant purpose of reducing tax. And if there are complex structures, there should be a commercial reason why they are complex.

This will apply to you if you run a professional firm. The ATO's definition of this is: "'Professional firms' offer customised, knowledge-based services to clients in a variety of professions which include, but are not limited to, accounting, architecture, engineering, financial services, law, medicine and management consulting."

This is extremely detailed guidance from the ATO, but broadly there are 3 things to consider:

- How much profit is taxed in the hands of the individual professional practitioner;

- Total effective tax rate of the profit generated from the business; and

- Remuneration for the practitioner v the benchmark or market rate for the services they provide the business.

For each of these three things, there is a points system the ATO give to assess its risk of falling into tax avoidance. If this applies to you, ideally you work closely with your accountant when it comes to tax planning time and work out who gets what profit from the business.

## Capital Gains Tax

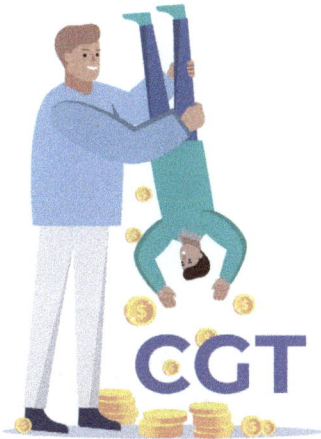

Capital gains tax or CGT is a tax you pay when you sell what is called a CGT asset. CGT assets encompass lots of things, including your own home. But in many cases, there are exclusions or concessions. For instance, while your home is a CGT asset, there is a "main residence exemption" that may apply to reduce any Capital gains tax you might pay on your home to $0.

You need to keep this in mind whenever you're going to sell a CGT asset, but they are commonly investments, such as property, businesses, shares, units in a trust, management funds, cryptocurrency – there's heaps of things that may attract CGT if you sell. The best thing to do before you sell an asset is to confirm the capital gains tax result on it beforehand and determine if there's any exemptions or concessions available to you.

The most common and well-known concession is the 50% general CGT discount — where if you own an asset for longer than 12 months, you receive a 50% discount to the amount of gain that you're taxed on. So say you make a $100,000 gain on selling a property, instead of paying tax on the $100,000 in total, if you're eligible, you'll only pay tax on $50,000 of it. This discount is only available to individuals or trusts (not companies).

## Capital Gains Tax — Small Business concessions

There are an additional set of CGT concessions for small business owners. You may be eligible for these selling a business, or selling assets related to a business that you run. There are four concessions that you may be able to use to reduce or remove any tax payable on a business sale. They are applied in a specific order and may reduce your taxable gain to $0. These are some of the most generous tax rules I know of, and I believe they were brought in to help and encourage small business ownership.

### Basic eligibility

Basic eligibility tests of having either an aggregated turnover of less than $2,000,000 or maximum net assets of under $6,000,000. Maximum net assets is tested on total net value of CGT assets owned by you, entities connected with you, affiliates, and entities connected with your affiliates. There's a ton of rules here, and there's plenty of exempt assets (such as personal use assets, your own home, and even your super balance). Where the turnover of the business being sold is close to or over $2,000,000, this is the test we look to confirm basic eligibility on. If you are relying on these rules when selling a business, it's important to get advice around this.

If you are selling shares in a company, an interest in a trust, or other indirect business, such as a company you own selling a business, there are additional tests which must be passed for that entity or the asset you sell to be eligible for the concessions. Once you have satisfied your basic eligibility, you can look to apply the four concessions. I'll run through these in the order that they must be applied.

In the examples below, let's say you sold a business with no cost to set up for a round figure of $3,000,000.

## 15-year complete exemption

You can completely ignore a gain if you meet the following criteria:

- You or the significant individual (if a company or trust) is 55 years or older and the event happened in connection with your retirement (or permanently incapacitated).

- You continuously owned the CGT asset for the 15-year period ending just before the CGT event happened.

This is the ultimate one to pass because it completely removes any CGT payable. If you ran the business for more than 15 years and were over 55, you could ignore any tax on the $3,000,000 gain. Keep in mind, using the remaining three concessions means that you will not have been eligible for this one.

## 50% Active Asset Reduction

This is a reduction of your gross gain by 50%. You can stack these concessions, and even stack it on top of the 50% general CGT discount if you own the asset more than 12 months. Unlike the general CGT discount, you can apply this discount in individuals, trusts, or companies.

What that means is, so far, a $3,000,000 gain on a business held for more than 12 months — you could reduce it by 50% to $1,500,000 by the general CGT discount (assuming it is held in a trust), then a further 50% active asset reduction down to $750,000.

## Small Business Retirement Exemption

You can claim the retirement exemption up to a lifetime limit of $500,000. If you have a net gain of less than $500,000, you will use a portion of your lifetime limit, with the remaining still being able to be offset for future gains. If your net gain is more than $500,000, you will use your whole lifetime exemption in one hit. No capital gains tax will be payable on amounts offset by the retirement exemption.

If you are under 55 years old, you will need to pay the amount of retirement exemption that you use into a complying super fund. Make sure you notify your fund of the special type of contribution it is — there is an election form. If you are over 55, you are not required to forward the amount to super. In the example I'm giving of the $3,000,000 gain, the previous concession took the net gain down to $750,000. If we apply this retirement exemption, our gain further reduces to $250,000.

## Rollover concession

The final of the 4 concessions is the rollover concession. This is where you purchase a qualifying replacement asset and can defer the gain of the amount you purchase a replacement asset with. Unlike the other concessions, this concession is a deferral and not an exemption or reduction in your gain. The entity selling the original small business asset must make the acquisition of the replacement asset. This can catch people out.

The replacement asset must be purchased between 1 year prior or 2 years after the date of the last CGT event in the income year in which you obtained this rollover. There are special timing rules if you have earnout agreements. If you expect to purchase a replacement asset but you do not do so within the required time, you will pay capital gains tax in the income year, of which the time to buy that replacement asset has run out. It's worth noting that the ATO can grant an extension to this time as well.

To follow on from my example, if we have a net gain of $250,000 to deal with after applying the previous concessions, and you buy a qualifying replacement asset for $200,000, you'll only defer $200,000 of the total $250,000 capital gain until you eventually sell the replacement asset.

## Concluding my example

So in my example, after using all 4 concessions, the net gain to deal with is now $50,000: the entity that made the gain will need to pay capital gains tax on that $50,000. If it is a trust, it can distribute the gain to the business owner. To give an idea, we would calculate the tax on the gain at the individual's marginal tax rate. If we used 39% as an example, the tax on a $3,000,000 gross gain before concessions would be $19,500. Pretty cool, hey?

## Division 7A (and solutions!)

Division 7A is a reference to the income tax legislation, and it applies to money that is owed to companies by shareholders of the company. The quick version of the rules say that money cannot be taken out of a company, unless a compliant loan is created and minimum repayments with interest are made. It also applies to trust distributions allocated to a company beneficiary by a trust, but have not yet been paid. We call these unpaid present entitlements or UPEs.

This situation usually comes about because the individuals in a family group take out more profit than they are personally taxed on. This could be for buying assets, investments, or living expenses with money that was originally in a company or otherwise owed to a company. If your loans or UPEs are not compliant, then per Division 7A rules, the amount of the loan or UPE is treated as an unfranked dividend. This could cause a massive amount of tax payable, depending on the situation.

So what are the solutions then? There are many, and it depends on the severity and scale of the loans you have to a company.

## The loans aren't all bad

They're not all bad, and sometimes we use them if there are big differences in taxable incomes each financial year — to balance them out or, sometimes, there's just a need for short term loans from a company. So first of all in the list of solutions, I want you to know that sometimes they're useful and to not think you have to get rid of them ASAP.

## Set up a loan agreement and make minimum repayments

The most basic solution is to set up a loan agreement and make repayments accordingly. You can create an unsecured loan for a maximum of 7 years. There is also the ability to create a secured loan agreement (on property, meeting certain loan to value requirements) which means you can have a 25-year loan. This will mean the annual repayments are much less than a 7-year loan. There is an ATO prescribed interest rate which changes each year. The ATO publish it each year, and the current rate for the 2024 financial year is 8.27%.

**IMPORTANT NOTE:** There is a fairly common strategy of parking money in an offset account for most of the year, then transferring it back late June as a repayment, then loaning it back in early July. This does not technically count as a loan repayment, and is not a solution to Division 7A. It is on the ATO's radar, so please do not do it even if it is what you have been advised.

So what are some common solutions to taking the pressure off Division 7A loans?

## Use Cascading Loans

It is possible to have a new loan agreement each year where you take drawdowns from the company. As accountants, we can record these as separate loans, separate agreements, with separate repayments on the balance sheet.

## Use a secured loan

As I mentioned earlier, if you have the equity in a property, you could create a secured loan. The benefits here are a longer loan term, so fewer minimum repayments are owed each year.

## Use dividends to pay the minimum repayment

If there is not enough cash to make the minimum repayment, it is possible to issue a dividend to the shareholders, but instead of paying the dividend in cash, it can be allocated to the Division 7A loan as a minimum repayment.

## Pay the cash into the company as full repayment of the loan

This could be used where the family group has access to cash and wants to put it in the company to build up savings for later use or to deploy within the company, such as investing in managed funds. Please note that I wouldn't recommend investing in the name of a company that also runs a business for asset protection purposes.

## Transfer assets into the company

Similar to cash, the family group could transfer business assets such as cars or other equipment or even existing investments like shares or managed funds through off-market transfers into the company.

Please note that when assets are transferred, the original owner is technically disposing of the asset, so capital gains tax needs to be considered on the transfer — along with stamp duty on certain assets when they are transferred even between related parties.

## Pay the top up tax

If there are limited ways above to help with Division 7A and the plan is to remove or repay it asap, you could explore just paying the "top up tax". What I mean is the difference between the company's franked dividend rate and the rate the individuals would get taxed on at their marginal rates. To illustrate this, your company might be franked at 25%. This franking credit is passed on as a prepaid tax. Imagine this goes to a shareholder that is paying tax at 39% on each dollar of dividend it receives, then the top up tax would be the difference between 39% and 25%, which is a top up tax of 14%.

It's also worth noting that the dividend may push the shareholder into a higher tax bracket, depending on how big the dividend is. It's best to do this with an accountant who can estimate the top up tax with accuracy so you can make an informed decision.

### Use a company as an investment vehicle

A solution that means you've always got a capped "flat" tax rate of 30% is to use a company as an investment vehicle. Often we look to invest via trusts because of their access to the capital gains tax discount of 50% if they hold an asset for longer than 12 months.

For high-income earning families, the tax rate individually might be from 39 to 47% anyway. So where we look to pay 50% of a high 47% tax rate on a big capital gain held in a trust, you're looking at a net tax of 23.5%. If we compare that to a bucket company at 30% with no CGT discount, that's only a 7% difference.

The benefit of investing via the company, though, is further avoiding Division 7A issues if there is money owed to a company in that family group.

## Restructuring your business

We've had situations where the business structure needs changing due to growth in the business, succession from one generation to the next, or allowing for investment. This has resulted in an opportunity during the restructure to consider how it may impact on Division 7A. There have been some great outcomes here, where the market value of the business or entity is essentially a loan owing to a trust or individuals in the family group from a company – which is a fantastic outcome for Division 7A purposes.

If you'd like to discuss this further, please book in for a strategy call and be sure to mention restructuring.

## GST Margin Scheme — for property developers

The GST margin scheme usually relates to property developers and is a great way to reduce the amount of GST they pay on their developments. It is not something that is automatically applied, like the rules generally around claiming and paying GST. It is something that property developers need to "tick the box on" if they are eligible to use it on the sale contract when they are selling land or new residential property.

Without it, a developer would ordinarily pay GST on the full sale price of the property they are selling, and one-eleventh would go to the ATO in the form of GST. The claim for GST would only be limited to GST on expenses incurred from costs involved in the construction or civil works involved in the production of the finished property. There would ordinarily be no GST claimable if the developer purchased the initial land or property they developed from a private buyer, which is very common. This can often make development uncommercial to carry out.

The margin scheme gives the same effect of claiming GST on the initial purchase, regardless of whether it had GST on it. Another way to put it simply, and why it's called the "margin" scheme, is that the calculation for how much GST to pay is to calculate the profit or margin you make on developing the property and paying GST only on that profit or margin.

I would recommend exploring whether or not you would be eligible for the margin scheme before you enter into a contract to purchase or as part of your due diligence. You do not want this to be a surprise cost in your development.

## Negative Gearing — property investors

Negative gearing is a term used to describe where an investment makes a tax loss, and you get a tax benefit as a result of that tax loss. It is usually used when referring to property investments. The situation arises in property where the rent received, less the tax-deductible cash outlays, less the non-cash tax deductions such as depreciation mean that the property is at a tax loss.

You can have instances where you have a cashflow positive but negatively geared property too. This would mean the non-cash tax deductions are significant, like the ones attached to depreciation especially in newly constructed dwellings that allow you to claim a higher depreciation.

It's not necessarily a bad thing, nor is it always a good thing to have negative gearing. There are some financial people that live by it and others that hate it. We're indifferent to it, and see it helps cashflow in a lot of circumstances.

When you're investing in property, and to assist with maximising your tax deductions, it's almost always best to get a tax depreciation report from a licensed quantity surveyor. This provides your accountant with the exact numbers they are able to claim when it comes to depreciation on your property.

If you are an employee and have a negatively geared property, you can also lodge a PAYG withholding variation with the ATO that allows your employer to withhold a lesser amount of tax when they pay you each payroll. This allows you to bring forward the tax refund you would otherwise receive when you lodge your tax return, and use this money for whatever purpose sooner.

## Part 4A

Part 4A refers to a section of tax law to do with tax avoidance. It's a bit of a buzz word that accountants use to describe behaviour, schemes, or strategies that do not align with tax law and may result in the ATO taking action on a taxpayer or tax agent they believe is operating outside the law. This is important to be aware of as the ATO have powers and responsibilities to ensure that taxpayers and tax agents are doing things correctly. You must operate within these rules and if you're working with a great accountant or tax agent they will be able to help you avoid breaking rules.

If you ever feel like advice you've received is suspicious or doesn't sound right, I would suggest getting a second opinion on whatever concerns you from another accountant or a tax lawyer if the situation needs it.

# Conclusion

I hope you've enjoyed reading this book as much as I have enjoyed developing it over the many years of running Inspire and the many workshops, webinars, and events that we've run with business owners.

Also if some or all of the contents in this book seems intense or hard to implement, please hear me with the right help, it's easy. Ensure you're working with an accountant who understands the strategies and ideas shared within this book.

While we're on the topic of accountants, my concern is that sometimes we are pigeon-holed into a certain service, such as only able to provide help doing tax returns. Depending on the accounting firm, this is an incorrect assumption and there are many ways we can add value to the journey of a business owner.

Consider two ways – the first being helping business owners better understand their numbers. How to control cash, grow profits and smash business valuations out of the park. It's not something business owners are often taught, and my book Total Financial Control goes into detail on our philosophies we share with our clients on this topic. The second is using the cash generated from a well-performing business and investing that into the family's wealth. Most accountants may not be financial planners themselves, but are able to guide you in the right direction to implementing wealth-creating strategies whether that's in the structures set up for you or introductions to people who can assist with exactly what to invest into. My book Wealth for Life goes further into how we achieve this at Inspire.

I would also love to hear any feedback you have about the book and the changes you've made as a result of the ideas and suggestions shared. Please feel free to connect with me on social media! My handle on Facebook, Instagram, and LinkedIn is 'benwalkerca'.

If you'd like to learn more about these tax strategies (and many others), please read Inspire's newsletter. You can subscribe on our website http://inspire.accountants. We hold many workshops and webinars on different topics, and the lens we look through is the lens of business owners.

So, from here on, please enjoy implementing these strategies to make sure you're on the right track to have your tax all sorted. If we master this as business owners, we'll have more mental energy and spare cash from paying the right amount of tax to reinvest into our family's lives, and in our local communities.

# Do you want to learn more about my accounting firm, Inspire?

Thanks again for reading my book, and hope you enjoyed it.

If you'd like to explore more about my accounting firm Inspire – Life Changing Accountants, please head to our website at https://inspire.accountants/

Got a problem with Tax, Your Accountant or Business Structures? The solution is a rapid fire Q & A session with an Inspire Accountant.

Book a phone call or a zoom chat with one of accountants, by heading to https://inspire.accountants/chat - or you can use the QR Code below.

The most common problems people reach out for are:

- A feeling that you might be paying too much tax
- Wanting to Change Accountants
- Needing to set up a NEW business structure
- Understanding your existing structure
- Considering the move to Xero
- Getting up to date with your TAX
- That the ATO is on your back
- Pulling more cash out of your business
- Finding ways to boost your profits
- Not knowing your numbers

# Acknowledgements

I want to acknowledge and send my gratitude to:

- My loving wife who has been there with me from before Inspire was even an idea. Thank you for the support and creating this beautiful thing called life and family together with me... Love you!

- My parents, Trish & Jeff, for being such a loving and supportive support. You gave me so many opportunities growing up and supported me with getting Inspire off the ground (at the detriment of accelerating the growth of your grey hairs!).

- My grandfather, who passed away a few years ago, for his inspiration of being able to step back from business to take care of my grandmother when she got cancer. That was an eye opener to me of how creating a business can give you options in life and allow you to put your family first.

- The awesome team at Inspire. Without you, the vision for Inspire would still be a dream. Now, we're living it.

- The hundreds of clients I've worked with from the start of Inspire where I have seen your journey growing your own business, wealth, and families.

- To all the partners of Inspire who help to implement strategies to provide great outcomes for our clients.

- To you, reading this book: thank you for giving up a few hours of your life to read my philosophies. I hope it was a worthwhile investment and remember: The Power of Any Idea is only in its implementation (Thanks to my mentor Paul Dunn, for that one!).

- To Emily Gowor who helped me through the process of getting another book to print. Thanks so much for making my publishing dream become a reality!

# About The Author

Ben Walker founded *Inspire – Life Changing Accountants* at the age of 23 with nothing but a borrowed printer, a laptop, and a simple idea. What if, instead of just doing tax and reporting on history, accountants could give game-changing advice that could help people create a better future for their business and their family?

Years on, *Inspire* has been showcased as a global example of what an accounting firm should be. This is thanks to Ben's disruptive approach to throwing out timesheets and charging by the hour, his challenge of the traditional 'old school' model of the accounting industry, and his belief that accountants change lives: their own lives, their team's, their clients, and others around the world.

Ben is a winner of the coveted *Anthill Online 30under30 Award*, was named a finalist in the *Brisbane Young Entrepreneur of the Year, Australian Accounting Award's*

*Mentor of the Year, Boutique Firm of the Year* and *Marketing Program Of The Year* for 2022. He has been featured in many publications including the *Courier Mail, Dent Podcast* with Glen Carlson, *Small Business Big Marketing* Podcast with Tim Reid, *Brisbane Business News & B Mag*.

Ben has also been a Chartered Accountant for more than a decade, and is the Author of multiple books. Today, while he continues to lead Inspire as Chartered Accountant & Founder, Ben's goal is to inspire others create a business that gives them the freedom to put family first and make a positive difference in the world.

TO BOOK BEN FOR A SPEAKING ENGAGEMENT,
FIND OUT MORE AT benwalker.com

TO EXPLORE WORKING WITH INSPIRE
VISIT inspire.accountants

# Other Books By Ben Walker

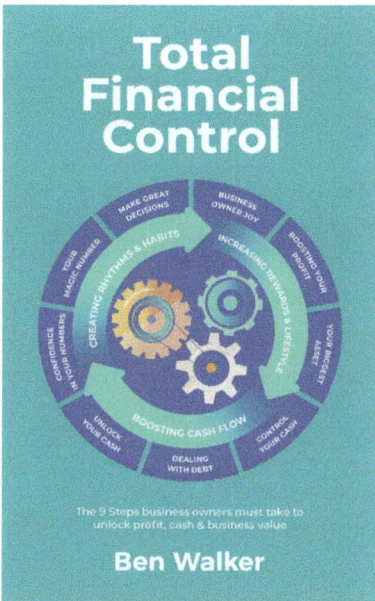

*Total Financial Control*

The 9 Steps business owners must take to unlock profit, cash & business value.

In this book, we share three key ideas through our 9 Step Method:

- Understanding what drives you and how that feeds your growth of profit and business value

- Boosting your cash flow to make it work for you and using debt to your advantage

- Building in the rhythms and habits required to create a high level of financial performance

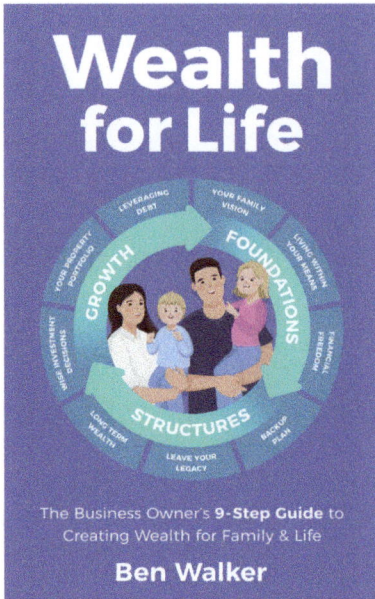

Wealth for Life

The Business Owner's 9-Step Guide to Creating Wealth for Family & Life

Ben Walker

## *Wealth for Life*

The Business Owner's 9-Step Guide to Creating Wealth for Family & Life.

In this book, we share three key ideas through our 9 Step Method:

- The foundations that you need to lock in as a family to provide a base for growing wealth

- The structures to implement to ensure

- Building in the rhythms and habits required to create a high level of financial performance